SELECTED POEMS

LINDLEY WILLIAMS HUBBELL
SELECTED BOOKS AND PAMPHLETS

POETRY PUBLISHED IN THE U.S.A.

Dark Pavilion (Yale University Press, 1927)
The Tracing of a Portal (Yale University Press, 1931)
Winter-Burning (Alfred A. Knopf, 1938)
The Ninth Continent (pamphlet, Alan Swallow, 1947)
Long Island Triptych and Other Poems
(Alan Swallow *&* William Morrow, 1947)
Seventy Poems (Alan Swallow, 1965)

POETRY FROM IKUTA PRESS (KOBE)

Autobiography (pamphlet, 1971)
Atlantic Triptych (1971)
Double Triptych (1974)
Climbing to Monfumo (1977)
Walking Through Namba (1978)
Czerny (pamphlet, 1982)
The First Architect (1982)

LITERARY STUDIES

Lectures on Shakespeare (Nan'un-dō, 1958)
Shakespeare and Classic Drama (Nan'un-dō, 1962)
Studies in English Literature (Yamaguchi Shoten, 1982)

SELECTED POEMS

Lindley Williams Hubbell

edited and with an introduction by Paul Rossiter

afterword by Yoko Danno

ISOBAR
PRESS

Published in 2025 by

Isobar Press
Sakura 2-21-23-202, Setagaya-ku,
Tokyo 156-0053, Japan

&

14 Isokon Flats, Lawn Road,
London NW3 2XD, United Kingdom

https://isobarpress.com

ISBN 978-4-907359-50-8

COVER IMAGES
Kazimir Malevich (1879–1935), *Suprematist Composition*, 1915;
author photograph by Donald Richie.

THANKS
I've been very grateful throughout this project for the kind-
ness and support of Yoko Danno and Hiroaki Sato, both of
whom were mentored early in their careers by Lindley Williams
Hubbell; sincere thanks also to David Burleigh, who generously
shared his knowledge of Hubbell, and who commented most
helpfully on the drafts of the editorial material. Any remaining
errors are, of course, my own.

– PAUL ROSSITER

CONTENTS

INTRODUCTION

INTRODUCTION

Lindley Williams Hubbell (1901–1994) is one of the forgotten figures of twentieth-century American poetry. The Library of America anthology, *American Poetry: The Twentieth Century, Volume Two*, which prints selections from the work of more than a hundred and twenty poets from E. E. Cummings to May Swenson, includes five pieces by Hubbell, but apart from this minimal representation, he is almost entirely lost to view. This is in spite of the fact that early in his career he had received a Yale Younger Poets Award for his first book, *Dark Pavilion* (1927), and that thereafter – as the depth and range of his work increased – he was published by Yale University Press for a second time (*The Tracing of a Portal*, 1931), and then by the prestigious publishers Alfred A. Knopf (*Winter-Burning*, 1938), and William Morrow and Alan Swallow, who in 1947 jointly published *Long Island Triptych and Other Poems*, perhaps Hubbell's most significant book, and certainly a work of considerable strength and originality.

There are a number of possible reasons for his later invisibility, but perhaps the major one is that in 1953, at the age of 52, he moved to Japan, took Japanese citizenship and a Japanese name (Hayashi Shūseki), and thereafter never returned to America. His fifth full-length collection, *Seventy Poems*, which included both the final poems he wrote in America and his earliest poems with Japanese settings, was published in Denver by Alan Swallow in 1965, but after this his work appeared exclusively in Japan, mostly with Ikuta Press, a small press run by poet Yoko Danno in Kobe. This press published five full-length volumes of Hubbell's poetry, three collections of his prose, and nine pamphlets of poems and translations. Apart from the second half of *Seventy Poems*, everything written by Hubbell after his arrival in Japan was published by Ikuta, the only exceptions being his volumes of literary criticism – although these too were published by Japanese, not American, presses. In other words, after 1953, Hubbell had no physical presence in the United States, and then after 1965 no published presence either.

He was not of course invisible to his friends, colleagues, students or former students in Japan, all of whom seemed to have greatly liked and respected him, but in terms of international recognition his invisibility has continued to this day. Obscurity of this kind seemed to have been something he didn't mind at all. No doubt he had had artistic and literary ambitions while he was living in the United States – perhaps even quite lofty ones – but in the state of mind he had attained after settling in Japan, it seems that that was no longer the important thing. His priorities appear to have been to engage with art, literature and theatre, and to be happy. Until slowed by the incapacities of age in his last few years, he cheerfully continued to read, write and teach, to attend performances of nō plays, and to sit in the front row at every concert he could get to by the Japanese pop idol Hashi Yukio. When he arrived in Japan, he hadn't necessarily planned to stay, but he liked it so much that he did. He was in a place where it was easy for him to be happy, and he never looked back:

> Around the hotel the autumn wind wails
> Continually.
> The room is chilly, winter is closing in,
> But all is well with me.

This was written on a visit to the ancient capital of Nara ('more than twelve centuries old,' the poem notes approvingly) quite early during his time in Japan, but his decision that Japan was where he wanted to be never wavered thereafter.

Moving so abruptly to an entirely new life in a never-before-visited country at the age of 52 – and a country culturally as different from the U.S.A. as Japan – is certainly a startling thing to have done and is interesting in itself; but what is just as remarkable is his now almost forgotten poetry. Hubbell wrote consistently for about sixty years, published ten full-length collections and seven pamphlets, and moved through several stylistic phases while always maintaining his own recognisable identity as a poet. He began in New York in the 1920s, where he wrote short, finely cadenced lyrics in the style of that city in that era: the poems are personal, and mostly concerned with love, betrayal, loneliness and mortality. Then, after what seems to have been a period of personal crisis in the mid-thirties, his range expanded enormously, whether that expansion is seen in terms of subject matter, form, technique or scale: *Long Island Triptych*, in particular, is a substantial modernist work with a wide range of historical, geographical, sociological, philosophical, zoological and streetwise reference, all carried off with great technical bravura. Finally, after his arrival in Japan, he moved to a more relaxed, anecdotal, everyday, and often humorous mode, albeit without slackening his attention to issues of technical and linguistic precision.

Throughout his career his poems are more various, in terms of both style and subject matter, than this division into three phases may suggest: his oeuvre includes, for example, both sharply written denunciations of racism and the human propensity for cruelty, and skilful (and often very funny) light verse. Nevertheless, the broad division into three periods is, I think, helpful in understanding his stylistic odyssey, so this introduction, in the course of describing Hubbell's life and poetry in more detail, will also try to say who or what at each stage might have influenced Hubbell to develop in the way that he did.

STARTING OUT

Lindley Williams Hubbell was born in Hartford, Connecticut, on 3 June 1901. His father, as Hubbell explained in a late interview with Yoko Danno in 1994, was an army officer, rarely present at home and 'only interested in hunting and fishing'. Hubbell nevertheless felt he was a good father: 'To me he was very kind, he never scolded me in his life. I was always left free, and to me he was very generous with money' ('Interview', 57). His mother was passionate about theatre in general and Shakespeare in particular, and Hubbell was only eight years old when he began reading the complete works of Shakespeare. By the age of ten, he told Yoko Danno in the same interview (58), he had not only read all the plays but had also memorised them. This education in drama continued into his teens, when his mother took him to see the many performances of Shakespeare put on in Hartford; mother and son also made frequent trips to New York to see plays, opera and ballet. As a result of this, Hubbell at an early age was able to see some of the great performing artists of that era: Eleanora Duse (a key figure for him all his life), Sarah Bernhardt, and Nijinsky, among many others. His teachers were less than happy about his absences from school, but his mother told them that it was 'more important for that boy to see Shakespeare than it is to come here' (59). Eventually – as he told Ueno Hisako, a close friend who cared for him in his final illness – after he had been at high school for only about two years, his mother asked him if he was learning anything there; when he said no, she immediately allowed him to leave (Ueno, 41). His formal education – including in Latin, Greek and Provençal – was thereafter in the hands of private tutors.

Both parents thus allowed him great freedom, and his mother encouraged his interest in art, literature and theatre. The decisive influence in his youth nevertheless seems to have been his 'aunt', Laura Williams. She was not in fact a blood relative but a neighbour and intimate of his mother; she was a cultured, cosmopolitan lieder singer, who had studied in Germany and lived in Italy. Hubbell told Yoko Danno that he mostly stayed at her home, where she tutored him in French, Italian, and German, and that she was the greatest influence in his life: she was the reason he used Williams as his middle name ('Interview', 57). By the time he left Hartford for New York many of his fundamental traits – his erudition, his love of language and languages, and his love of theatre and the other performing arts – were well established.

Once in New York, after a year-long foray into acting as a junior member of the theatre company led by the eminent Shakespearean Robert Mantell, Hubbell, relying on his father's generosity, did very little until in 1925 he began a job in the Map Room of the New York Public Library; apart from two extended leaves of absence, he remained there until 1946. But it was presumably during the early 1920s that he wrote the poems that went into his first book, *Dark Pavilion*. Judging from the content of these poems – baffled desire, romantic misunderstanding, betrayal, loneliness, the destruction of beauty by time (with hardly a word about New York as a lived-in city) – Hubbell was not a happy young man. The poems are, however, crafted with a degree of skill that clearly provided its own consolation – and further consolation must have been forthcoming when the book received a Yale Younger Poets Award and was published by Yale University Press in 1927.

An example of Hubbell's manner in *Dark Pavilion* is 'Remember This':

Remember this, O pitiful heart:
As surely as lover and lover part,

So do a man and his sorrow take
Divergent paths, for healing's sake.

Remember this, O haunted mind:
The years are slow but certainly kind;
And every grief and every crime
Will seem less terrible, in time.

Most of the features of his early work are in place here: the subject of loss, the small scale, the stanzaic parallelism, the iambic flow, the crisp rhymes, the mastery of cadence. The placing of the comma in the last line seems exactly right: with no punctuation the line would be flat, while with heavier punctuation – a dash, say – the line would sound portentous. The light pause created by the comma articulates the emotion, the not-yet-achieved reconciliation to loss, very exactly.

Such precisions mean that the poems, even when focused on auto-biographical distress, rarely descend to self-pity, instead articulating and containing the emotion within achieved metrical forms. In this they show some similarity to work by his contemporaries – especially his woman contemporaries – in 1920s New York, poets who, in the words of Richard Gray, 'used formal structures to channel and intensify feeling' (Gray, 189), and 'whose work demonstrates a vivid contrast between the intensely personal, subjective nature of their subjects and the extraordinarily polished, objective character of the poetic forms they use' (191). Among these poets might be counted the slightly older Elinor Wylie (1885–1928) and Edna St. Vincent Millay (1895–1950) – whose second volume *A Few Figs from Thistles* (1920) had established her as the unofficial poet laureate of the Jazz Age – and perhaps Louise Bogan (1897–1970) or Leonie Adams (1899–1988). All these poets were active in New York in the 1920s. Hubbell certainly knew Wylie's work – he quotes a couplet of hers in a 1969 letter to Yoko Danno ('Letters', 4), and he spoke highly of Millay's work in a letter to the editor of the *New York Times* in the 1920s (Wise, 171-172) – but as far as I know he otherwise only mentioned these writers in passing. It does nevertheless seem likely that as a young poet living in New York he read their key books as they appeared during the course of the decade.

One year in particular – 1923 – was an exceptionally active twelve months in New York poetry publishing: Elinor Wylie's second book, *Black Armour,* and Louise Bogan's first, *Body of This Death,* both appeared in that year, and *The Harp-Weaver and Other Poems* by Edna St. Vincent Millay won the Pulitzer Prize. However, there was another impulse also in play: in addition to books by these more traditional and formalist poets, two major volumes of modernist poetry were published in New York in that year, *Spring and All* by William Carlos Williams and *Harmonium* by Wallace Stevens. Hubbell had certainly read the second of these by the time he used a phrase from it as the title of his second book, *The Tracing of a Portal* (1931), even if Stevens's influence is not otherwise very noticeable in his work. Later in life, he discussed Williams's work in his essay 'Poetry and Prose in Modern Literature', published in 1975 in *A Second Miscellany* (87-89, 115-116), and in a letter in the 1980s he told David Burleigh that Williams had been an important influence ('One of the Few', 30). There is, however, little sign of Williams's influence in his early work even if, by the time he was writing his essays in the 1950s, he clearly knew Williams's work well. It seems likely that as his engagement with the New York formalist poets waned and that of Williams waxed, the quotidian and observational aspects of the early work of Williams began to be an influence on his late poems of everyday life in Japan.

Thus, even though the decade of the 1920s was a classic era for modernism, and even though Hubbell himself always spoke of his respect for the poetic masterpieces published at this time on the other side of the Atlantic – Ezra Pound's *Hugh Selwyn Mauberley* (1920) and T. S. Eliot's *The Waste Land* (1922) – there are few signs of such high modernism in his first book, whose poems are stylistically closer to those of the women poets of New York than to the spiky modernisms of Williams, Pound and Eliot.

It seems clear, however, that Hubbell was also attuned to other, older traditions of formal verse than those displayed in the smart modernity of the New York poets who were his contemporaries. Judging by what he said and wrote later in his life, when he was reflecting on his past and his influences, it seems evident that the work of Emily Dickinson must have been a key influence. In the 1994 interview he told Yoko Danno that Dickinson was one of the five writers who had been most important to him, the others being Shakespeare, Ibsen, Homer, and Gertrude Stein

(65). It is easy to see how Dickinson's terseness, her control of cadence within the formal constraints of her quatrains, the sharpness of her lexical choices, and her use of rhyme would together have been influences on Hubbell's own early work.

Another fundamental influence was the Elizabethan and seventeenth-century English lyric tradition. In his *Studies in English Literature* (1982), the chapters on the English lyric in the sixteenth and seventeenth centuries – fifty pages and forty-six pages, respectively – are the longest in the book. In the chapter on seventeenth-century poetry Herrick is favoured with ten pages, the most devoted to any poet in the whole volume, and Hubbell declares that Robert Herrick 'is the best lyric poet in the language' (90). Herrick's work, Hubbell says, is 'so perfect [that] it is better to give examples than description' (94). This he then proceeds to do for a full five pages, offering numerous instances of Herrick's stanzaic virtuosity, technical skill, and delicacy.

The triangulation of the key features of the 1920s New York poets, Dickinson, and Herrick thus seems to have helped Hubbell to create his initial poetic language, one that he exploited with relish in his first two books. In the case of all three, smallness, wit, technical skill, and beauty of cadence were key features. In particular, his poems might best be compared with those of Elinor Wylie, who, David Perkins notes, sought to master a 'small, clean technique' and 'to turn out "brilliant and compact stanzas" comparable to "enamelled snuffboxes"' (Perkins, 375).

TRACING A PORTAL

Hubbell's second book, *The Tracing of a Portal* (1931), begins to expand the range of his work. The title of the book comes from a line in 'Peter Quince at the Clavier', a poem – much admired by Hubbell – from Wallace Stevens's first book, *Harmonium* (1923):

> Beauty is momentary in the mind –
> The fitful tracing of a portal.

In Hubbell's new book there is still the same lyrical emphasis as in *Dark Pavilion* – and indeed, similar emotions of longing and loss in many of the poems – but the title perhaps suggests a change of emphasis: rather than the darkened pavilion of the first book's title poem, presumably designed for pleasure but now fallen into disrepair, we are given a tentative limning – a 'fitful tracing' – of a possibly rather grand doorway that might allow entrance to some more fruitful place – or at least an exit from the confinement of the earlier book's ruin, where 'mine are the only ears that ever listen / When the bats knock and the rotten rafters fall'.

In *The Tracing of a Portal* there is, thematically speaking, no longer quite as much emphasis on loss as in the earlier book, and when there is loss, it is perhaps more often the result of transience and mortality than of romantic setbacks or personal betrayal. In addition, there are other intimations of the new in this book: there are some initial, tentative engagements with modernism, there is a greater variety of voice and tone, and for the first time New York begins to appear in Hubbell's work as actual presence and inhabited environment.

'Afternoon Ferry' is an example of the last of these:

> The rain fell slowly into the hushed city
>   And into the dark water of the bay.
> Gulls rode the tide on blocks of ice,
>   Gray upon gray.
>
> There was Hoboken ahead of me, and Union City,
>   And the rain wetting my face,
> And the boat plowing through water and broken ice
>   From one desolate place to another desolate place.

The mood of the speaker is unhappy enough, but at least the ferry between Manhattan and the New Jersey shore, and the dark water with the 'gulls [riding] the tide on blocks of ice', are actually seen, constituting both a described locality and an image that effectively embodies the speaker's emotional state: for the first time Hubbell's adopted city appears *in propria persona* in one of his poems. It is a poem of depression – a condition which Hubbell told Ueno Hisako he had intermittently suffered from throughout his life (Ueno, 39) – but avoids self-pity both by the concreteness of what is seen and described, and by the poem's formal precisions. For example, the doubling of the word 'gray' in the

last, two-stress line of the first stanza is echoed by the doubling of
'desolate' in the long last line of the second and final stanza: the lines
are of very different lengths, but this asymmetry is played off against the
parallel verbal repetitions, making for a conclusive but flexible symmetry
in the overall musical shape of the poem.

The city appears in an even more dramatic guise a few poems later
in a piece simply titled 'New York'. It begins, surprisingly enough, with
the city rising 'from the sea like an iron lily', and then goes on to develop
this simile, describing New York as 'the great lily, the lily of marble and
steel / Cutting the air with its petals', before concluding, 'surely the heart
is made whole that has beheld, / Perfect upon the stem, this flower.'
This is certainly unexpected both in terms of its spirit – given Hubbell's
usually rather down-hearted presence in his early work – and in terms
of such a simile having been chosen to describe this particular city in
the first place. It looks as if this poem – with its long lines, absence of
rhyme and self-conscious embrace of hardness and the metallic – is an
attempt on Hubbell's part to write himself out of a poetic universe of
grieving, dead leaves, winter storms, iambics, and tight formalism into a
new modernity or even modernism.

There were a number of influences working to move Hubbell in this
direction. In one of the short poems in the pamphlet *Autobiography*
(1971), Hubbell lists the three most memorable aesthetic high points in
his early life: hearing Mary Garden singing *Mélisande*; reading Gertrude
Stein's *Tender Buttons* for the first time; 'but most of all perhaps / The
time I went to see / At the Wildenstein / Brancusi's first show.' Gertrude
Stein, as will shortly become clear, was crucial to Hubbell's development,
but the abstract or modernist artists whose work he encountered in New
York were almost equally important. The impact of the work that Hubbell
saw at Brancusi's 1926 New York solo exhibition is well captured in the
first part of 'City of Islands' in his 1938 volume *Winter-Burning*. This
is an apocalyptic poem, imagining a very different New York from the
'great lily' that had appeared in 'New York'; the city in this later poem is
a place of impoverishment and filth, which at the end of the poem sinks
beneath the ocean 'in a whisper of foam'; the work of Brancusi is the only
redeeming feature in this dystopia. This encounter with Brancusi's work
seems to have been a turning point, and thereafter Hubbell's taste in the
visual arts (or in the twentieth-century art of the west, at any rate) was

strongly modernist in character. He later wrote important poems about Duchamp ('Porte-Bouteilles' in the 1947 volume *Long Island Triptych and Other Poems*), and about Malevich and Mondrian in *Seventy Poems* of 1965, a volume which also included images of paintings by these two artists.

In 1931 these articulations of his admiration for the great modernist artists were still in the future, however: it was too soon for him to be able to transform his style so radically, and he certainly doesn't do so in *The Tracing of a Portal*, where the lyrical, the rhymed, the cadenced, and the elegiac are dominant in almost every poem in the book. There are, however, two poems that point forward to Hubbell's later development. One of these is 'Line'. This poem, while still fastidious in its metre and rhymes, sheds many of the stage props of his lyrical style in favour of a condensed and abstract definition of the kind of style to be wished for, one that dispenses with the 'vehemence' of naturalistic colour in favour of the 'beauty of a naked line'; it is a kind of recipe for future artistic development, one that indicates a path towards the achievements to come in the 1940s.

> I would take all color,
> Watch it grow paler, duller;
> I would see it fade from the stem, and see it die
> Out of the morning sky and the evening sky.
> I would have the intricate curve
> Bent straight.
> I have come to hate
> All vehemence, the coarse tint and the fine.
> I would see all beauty in a naked line.

The other is the poem 'A Letter to Gertrude Stein'.

'THE MOTHER OF US ALL'

In spite of the fact that Hubbell never wrote anything that sounds remotely like Gertrude Stein, her example was crucial to him. As I suggest in my afterword to the reissue of *Long Island Triptych*, Hubbell's mid-length poem published in 1947, he did not in that work imitate any of the surface features of Stein's style; rather, it was her understanding – derived from her friendship with Picasso, and her long and close engagement with both his work and that of Cézanne – of how the methods and perspectives of Cubism could be applied to literary art that enabled the very individual modernism of Hubbell's most important poem. His modernism does not resemble that of any of the other high modernist writers who might have been candidates for the role of helping him transform his style; rather, he was able to invent his own form and his own way of proceeding, and it was almost certainly Stein's example that helped him to do that.

If this is so, it is difficult to over-estimate the importance of Stein and her work for Hubbell. The already quoted response to Yoko Danno's question in the 1994 interview about which five writers had meant most to him gives a sense of this importance, as does the mention in *Autobiography* of the first reading of *Tender Buttons* as one of the three aesthetic experiences that, at the age of seventy, he would most like to be able to relive. In a letter to Yoko Danno in 1971, Hubbell went so far as to claim that 'we have all been influenced by Gertrude Stein. She is "the Mother of us all."'('Letters', 9).

Hubbell first encountered Stein's work in the Spring 1922 issue of *The Little Review*. He was, he said in the 1994 interview, 'overwhelmed' – and was even more impressed when he went on to read *Tender Buttons* in the reading room of the New York Public Library. Dismayed by the fact that 'at that time all the writing about her was ridicule', Hubbell wrote a letter to Eugene Jolas, editor of the Paris magazine *transition*, praising him for printing Stein's work; Jolas showed this letter to Stein, who in turn wrote to Hubbell, saying, 'Mr Jolas has just shown me your letter to *transition*. It gave me a great deal of pleasure.' After this they corresponded regularly.[1] When Stein visited America for the first of her lecture tours, she contacted Hubbell, and she and Hubbell met frequently during her stay. In the introduction to *Everybody's Autobiography* Stein provides a glimpse of Hubbell as he was in 1934:

Lindley Hubbell had been for many years a comfort to me, he read all I wrote and he always told me warmly that he had. I had thought that he would be a tallish pale and sympathetic New

Englander. Not at all, he was short and dark and neat and prim and he attends to all the maps in the Astor library. (*Everybody's Autobiography*, 7)

From this time on Stein and Hubbell became firm friends as well as committed correspondents.

The piece by Stein in *The Little Review* that triggered this whole train of events was 'Vacation in Brittany', a short three-part work in prose. Here is the first part:

By the sea smell the goose, by the figs George buy the figs. By the crown, Sylvester has the crown and glory constant glory. And in the midst of the speed in the rising of the stones stones do not rise of themselves unless they are made to resemble the wood in the midst of stones and salt can we declare when a house was built. A house is built either in the shape of a lamb of a heart or of a bush. And almost immediately the walls scale. They whiten and the sun changes chinese red to blue.

Immerse yourself.

In contrast, Hubbell's 'Letter to Gertrude Stein' sounds like this:

The roots have struck deep: tree root and flower root and the
small absurd weed nourished by dust;
In this rich soil a whole generation that would have found
death in the wind and the black ice,
But the roots were fast, the loam was packed tightly about
them, the serried stalks were secure,
The earth was stronger than the deep ice, the earth gave back
laughter to the laughter of the wind, the ice cracked.

In the cities it was the same: people leaned out of windows
and sniffed the air and laughed,
Children flew past in a clatter of roller skates, children
screamed, their voices louder than the clatter of their skates,

> The older ones played ball in the streets, chairs were brought
> out on the pavements, women rocked back and forth,
> In all the cities it was like this, and in the little towns no one
> stayed in the houses when work was done.

Clearly, this does not sound like the early work of Stein; moreover, it doesn't sound like any other poem by Hubbell up to that point or to come later. What is extraordinary is not only the difference in style from that of the other poems in his first two books – not least in the use of long, Whitman-like lines – but also the nature of the vision. Hubbell's vision in his early work had been mostly sombre, even glum, but this sounds almost like a more quietly spoken version of the 'Revival of the Eternal Man' in the Ninth Night of Blake's *Vala, or the Four Zoas*:

> Let the slave grinding at the mill run out into the field
> Let him look up into the heavens & laugh in the bright air …
> And let his wife & children return from the oppressor's scourge:
> They look behind at every step & believe it is a dream …
> If you are thirsty there is the river, go bathe your parched limbs.
> The good of all the Land is before you for Mystery is no more!

Thus, even though Hubbell's poem is not stylistically like anything by Stein, it seems likely that she liberated something in him that enabled him to write a poem of a kind that he hadn't written before – and, moreover, a poem that expressed a kind of vision that he hadn't attempted to articulate before. The last lines of the third part of 'Vacation in Brittany' are: 'Let us let us conscience. Let us let us conscientiously renounce the sense of reticence.' It seems that perhaps Stein in some way gave permission to Hubbell – or encouraged Hubbell to give permission to himself – to renounce some of the 'neat and prim' reticence of the 'New England Puritan' that the first sentence of his 'Autobiography in Fifty Sentences' claims to have been the key to his identity, and thus enabled him to write the first poem in his career of unalloyed joy, of a spring that has fully arrived and is unrepentantly blossoming:

> The miracle was that sweetness was not gone out of the sap, that
> the stem was not ashamed to bear blossoms,

That the roots were glad of the rain, that the slow wind was
permitted gladly, that the boughs were fed willingly.

As Stein said: 'Immerse yourself.' Hubbell was to go on to write other
poems filled with joy later in his career, but this poem is the first of them,
and it seems to have been a breakthrough.

GEOMETRIC OSTRICHES

Hubbell's third book, *Winter-Burning* was published by Alred A. Knopf
in 1938; Hubbell thereby joined a prestigious list that included Elinor
Wylie, A. E. Housman, Wallace Stevens and Witter Bynner. *Winter-
Burning* is a transitional book: a number of the poems are similar in
style and content to previous work, but there are new things here also.
As before, there are short personal lyrics and sonnets, but both types
of poem show a new tautness of expression; other lyrics lightly but
neatly address philosophical or scientific issues ('the hypothesis / Of in-
organic life', or dualism versus monism, for example). There is a poem
about Ibsen; there is 'City of Islands' whose first part, registering the
impact of first seeing the work of Brancusi, has already been mentioned;
and there is a starkly atmospheric Arctic landscape poem ('Ellesmere
Island'), presumably a fruit of the month's holiday in Canada in 1932
that Hubbell reports to Stein.[2] There is also a poem ('Ostrich Vase, Pre-
Dynastic') claiming ancient Egyptian art was the earliest to behold 'the
line within the girth', thereby 'Filling eternity with these / Geometric
ostriches' – an insight that harks back to 'Line' in his previous volume
and looks forward to 'Reading History' in his next book, which speaks of

> Egypt before the Pharaohs came,
> where the painter of pots painted the abstract line
> in what he saw, and not the thing he saw.

And near the end of the volume there is a group of poems displaying a
striking sympathy for animals and other creatures, a theme that would
become increasingly important for Hubbell and later lead him to reprint
three poems from this volume – 'The Cats', 'The Insect Hospital at

Ahmedabad', and 'Tropical Fish in the Aquarium' – in his penultimate collection, *Walking Through Namba*, published forty years later in 1978. There they keep company with a small anthology of minimalist pieces about a menagerie of creatures: alligator, *suzumushi* ('bell insect'), rat, whale, pigeon, python, and others.

Perhaps the most unexpected novelty in *Winter-Burning*, though, is 'Three Letters'; these are lengthy, splendidly camp pastiches of translated Latin epistles:

> New gods from the east are dumped upon our wharves
> Like unfamiliar animals for the theatre.
> Even Antinous has become a god;
> The pretty boy from Bithynia that great Hadrian
> Used for a mattress, to whom
> The reverend senators and grave aediles burn
> A pinch of incense, laughing in their togas.

This is lively enough, and is perhaps the only occasion on which Hubbell clearly speaks through a mask. As David Burleigh points out in his 1991 essay, Hubbell does not generally

> make any use of personae in his writing so that, while he may compose in different tones and voices, these are all effectively his own. Nowhere does Hubbell create an imaginary voice or character, a dilatory Prufrock or exquisite Mauberley, but always retains his own essentially lucid manner. ('Defiant and Alone', 173)

These three letters constitute perhaps the only occasion on which this is not true – even if the first and second of them (though not the third) certainly display his 'essentially lucid manner'. This ventriloquial style was nevertheless not something that Hubbell followed up on; however complex some of the writing of his middle period became, the complexity is always fundamentally grounded in his own voice.

Although *Winter-Burning* was not published until 1938, it seems likely that the poems in it were written in the first part of the 1930s. It appears that in 1935 Hubbell had some kind of breakdown; fortunately, he was able to take time off from the library and, subsidised by a friend, visit Italy. This seems to have effected a cure. In his short memoir 'On First Meeting LWH', Donald Richie, who later lived for many years in Japan, becoming a leading expert on Japanese cinema, tells of his first meeting with Hubbell in 1943 in the Map Room of the New York Public Library. Richie had gone there because he was, he believed, about to be posted by the navy to Italy. 'Wouldn't it be nice if they sent you to Venice,' Hubbell said, and then added, 'Venice changed my life – it was the first place where I realized that one could be happy…. I don't mean not unhappy, you understand, a common enough state. I mean happy – a much rarer state' (Richie, 3). The restorative power of Hubbell's experience in Venice is celebrated in the first stanza of the poem 'Five Places' in his next book, *Long Island Triptych and Other Poems*. This five-stanza poem is a kind of spiritual autobiography in which each stanza describes the significance of a particular place in Hubbell's life. The respective stanzas begin: 'In Venice I was saved…. In San Juan I was purified…. In Halifax I was empty…. In 'Sconset I was filled…. In Perth Amboy, I was free.'[3] The complete first stanza reads:

> In Venice I was saved. The second birth
> Is not an event but a process. The scission in the psyche
> Must knit at last or split from end to end.
> I thought I was going to split but I knit instead.
> No, Mr. Hubbell, you're not going crazy,
> If you were you wouldn't ask me that question.
> We had breakfast on the balcony overlooking
> The Grand Canal, and late in the afternoon
> We went to Torcello to see the great golden Madonna
> And I got fleas on the ferry. On the further side
> Of the Giudecca, beyond the Dogana and the Salute,
> The backyards looked like backyards anywhere.
> People called to each other, their voices clear on the water.

A return from psychological crisis – with the help of a supportive companion, the great golden Madonna, and fleas – to the ordinariness, sociability and clarity of the everyday is movingly and unpretentiously captured here.

In a letter to Yoko Danno in 1986, Hubbell says: 'When I came back from Italy I didn't write any poetry for three years. When I started again my poetry had completely changed' ('Letters', 17). If Hubbell did no writing between his return from Italy in 1935 and the publication of *Winter-Burning* in 1938, it must be the case that the poems in the 1938 volume were written before he left on his restorative journey. And this fits well with the tone of *Winter-Burning* as a whole. The poems in this book don't sound like the work of someone at the end of his psychological and emotional tether: the personal poems are less directly unhappy than those with similar themes in the first two books, the subject matter is broader in range and is approached in a spirit of greater curiosity and objectivity, and, in 'Three Letters', there is the imaginative willingness to work with a lively persona.

Hubbell's next major publication, *Long Island Triptych and Other Poems*, published in 1947, seems to be the fruit of his poetic revival after his three-year silence, a revival that runs through to 1945, the year in which, according to the inner jacket of *Double Triptych* (1974) – an Ikuta Press book that prints *Long Island Triptych* and the later *Atlantic Triptych* (1971) in a single volume – the earlier triptych was composed.

ANGELS OVER BROOKLYN

Long Island Triptych and Other Poems, which starts with twelve formally various poems, together acting as a collective prologue to the complex mid-length title poem, is a confident, witty, virtuoso, and often powerful performance – one that announces Hubbell's arrival as a modernist poet with his own distinctive and consistent voice. These 'other poems' begin with a statement of Hubbell's modernist alignment in 'Porte-Bouteilles', a tribute to Marcel Duchamp – 'the purest eye / Since the industrial revolution' – who, by exhibiting a bottle rack created the first ready-made, a work which 'stands like a pharos / Over dark waters.'

This paean to the modern is immediately followed by a plunge deep into the Middle Ages in 'Angelology', a poem of nine tightly written thirteen-line stanzas in praise of the 'noble science of angelology'. The poem is a catalogue of the nine celestial orders – one stanza each for angels, archangels, principalities, powers, virtues, dominions, thrones, cherubim and seraphim. It includes mentions of the Persian origin of these celestial beings, various episodes in the history of the 'science' from the time of its ancient founding onwards, and descriptions of representations of angels from a number of different cultures and eras – but what is most striking about the poem is the way in which it is so deeply embedded in 1940s New York, where the angels are evidently continuing to operate at full strength:

> Archangels … loom past you
> As you sit drinking coffee in a booth.
> Above the powerful throat the bending head
> Looks thoughtful but is perhaps only beautiful.
> They never accept minor commissions, tots
> Lifted brusquely out of a traffic jam
> (Who was the nice person that carried me across the street,
> Mommy?) they bar the way with flaming swords,
> Wrestle with patriarchs, announce important births,
> And minister to men with little dogs.

Dominions, virtues and powers, on the other hand, 'sing / Glory to God, early and late':

> Sometimes they sing a trio or a duet,
> And sometimes all together, a capella,
> Or with the tromba marina, or with continuo
> On the clavicembalo,
> On trucks or waiting for trucks in alleys,
> Climbing subway stairs or waiting for subways
> Or walking down 42nd Street,
> A neat package tucked under the arm.

Thrones, meanwhile

> … have been over Brooklyn with chromium wings
> Reaching from the Pleiades to Orion's right foot,
> On clear nights they rise over Prospect Park,
> Over the WPA zoo, on the juke box
> Tex Ritter is singing Have I Stayed Away Too Long?

The juxtaposition in lines such as these of a tromba marina with trucks waiting in alleys, or angels in flight with Tex Ritter on the juke box, is a striking feature of this poem and foreshadows one of the key strategies of *Long Island Triptych* itself: time is seen as 'vertical', less as a horizonal flow than as a series of historical depths one below the other, all of which are felt to be simultaneously present in the lived experience of contemporary New York. As in *The Waste Land,* many places and times are felt to be vividly and simultaneously present and to be fully implicated in the experience of life in the modern city; here, however, in contrast to the despairing darkness of Eliot's poem, the spirit of such contemporaneity is a celebratory one:

> The seraphim afire flow above the river,
> The glory of God flows above the seraphim.
> Holy Holy Holy they sing,
> St. Louis Blues they sing, Blues in the Night they sing.
> My heart melts, the marrow in my bones melts.
> The glory goes over the city, through the Narrows,
> > past Ambrose Lightship.

In this combination of celebration, particularity, close observation, humour, juxtaposition and simultaneity Hubbell seems to have found his own distinctive voice.

After these strong beginnings, the 'other poems' section of the book goes on to include two retrospective poems, one from San Juan ('Lament for Puerto Rico') and one from Italy ('The Nightingales at Ca' Giupone') together with the autobiographical overview poem, 'Five Places', an excerpt from which has already been quoted. There is also 'Reading History', a powerful early statement of Hubbell's anti-racism, and 'Snow', a return, albeit with a new steadiness and maturity, to the formal lyric of romantic disappointment. The final poems in the section include an elegy for a blown-down tree ('The Blue Spruce') and a poem about a Chinese philosopher's appreciation of the 'living rock' in his garden which speaks 'only the one word / Of its identity' ('Mi Fei'). These motifs – trees and rock, and the attention and respect to be accorded them – will recur often in Hubbell's later work.

TRIPLE COUNTERPOINT

The key work in *Long Island Triptych and Other Poems*, however, is the title poem, a forty-eight-page poem in three parts.[4] Each panel of the triptych focuses on one of three New York neighbourhoods, Greenpoint (in Brooklyn), Ridgewood (in Queens), and Glendale (also in Queens) and consists of ten poems, each of which is formally distinct from the other nine. Two of the key strategies in this poem – juxtaposition and simultaneity – have already been deployed in 'Angelology', but perhaps the most striking thing about the poem is its overall architecture. The three panels of the triptych are perfectly parallel to each other in that they each consist of instances of the same ten poetic forms deployed in the same order; the matter dealt with in these different kinds of writing is very various, but this variety is contained within a robust structure of formal parallelism. Thus, not only are different people, species, works of art, religions, and historical – even geological – eras juxtaposed, but different poetic forms are similarly placed side-by-side in a way that at first seems arbitrary – in that it stresses the heterogeneity of the forms being used – but is not in fact haphazard in that similar forms appear in the same positions in all three panels of the triptych. In order to make this parallelism clear, it may be best to describe in some detail the sequence of different kinds of writing as they occur in 'Greenpoint', the first panel of the triptych, so as to illuminate the matrix to which all three parts conform.

The first part of the poem begins joyously at the start of day in Greenpoint:

> The Glory of God shines over Greenpoint.
> The oxen of the sun
> Tread out the darkness along Newel Street.

The first stenographer announces dawn.
The delicatessens open. It is day.

The juxtaposition of the Glory of God, the Homeric oxen of the sun, the named suburban New York street, the stenographer, and the delicatessens together sound a chord that brings together different times, persons, settings, and orders of reality in an urban harmony, and in doing so announces juxtaposition and simultaneity as important procedures of the poem. This brief opening chord is immediately followed by a poem of geographical description and historical narrative running from the sale of the land by the Canarsie Indians to the Dutch West India Company in 1638 through to the construction of the modern refineries, foundries, and warehouses – and to contemporary local Polish boys playing handball in the side yard of the St. Stanislaus Kostka Catholic Academy. Part III is a conversational poem in irregularly rhymed seven-line stanzas, a dialogue between the main speaker and someone called Rena, who plays much the same role as the person who assured Hubbell of his sanity in Venice; this time, however, there seems to be less need of reassurance as the speaker replies to Rena by saying, 'I don't wish I were dead / And I don't need a buffer / Between me and hell. / I'm doing all right. I'm getting along quite well.' Part IV is a disquisition on the human heart, on the distinction between the emotional and the intellectual nature, and on that between the poet and the mystic ('The poet aspires toward silence, the mystic achieves it'), with a supporting cast that includes among others Turgenev, Emma Goldman, Dorothy Richardson ('You never know which moment will be your next'), *Webster's Collegiate Dictionary* (Fifth Edition), Duchamp, Valéry, Rimbaud and Vivekananda.

I think it must already be clear that the poem is replete with different perspectives, poetic forms, orders of information, allusions, tones of voice, and emotional emphases. This carnival of juxtaposition reaches a climax in Part V, which is a double sestina, one of the most demanding poetic forms in the western tradition. In this case the form is being used to articulate nothing less than a history of mankind from various pre-Neanderthal species all the way through to the contemporary inhabitants of Greenpoint who 'frequent pool parlors [and] frequently … have / Tail in the park.' This virtuoso performance, the longest poem in the sequence, is immediately followed by one of the shortest, a lyric in three rhymed quatrains which returns to Newel Street to capture a moment of heart-breaking personal vision, and this is in turn followed by a tightly written, deeply personal poem of recovery from humiliation, self hatred, and bad living, and return to 'the sound within silence and the silence within sound / And light within darkness' (associated with the work of Brancusi and Mondrian) that constitutes 'the center of my being'. Part VIII is a plunge into deep prehistoric time, a brief poem in couplets about precursors to *Homo sapiens* who lived 'Before the ice sheet / Passed over Long Island', while Part IX is a kind of Socratic dialogue investigating human ignorance and indifference and the role of art in awakening imagination. After all this multi-faceted matter, whose sheer variety is representative of many aspects of Hubbell's life, thought, and preoccupations, this panel of the triptych ends with a short coda that returns us to a fragility earlier expressed in the lines in the San Juan stanza of 'Five Places' which speak of learning humility in the aftermath of breakdown, of the peril in saying 'this cannot happen to me again', and of the sense of 'walking the razor's edge from that time forth':

> In early middle age
> There comes a quiet time
> When you think the fight is won.
>
> It has not even begun.
>
> The fire roars in the wood,
> The tide rises higher
> Than you thought it ever could.

The first panel of the triptych thus includes a great variety of subject matter expressed in an equally great variety of formal procedures. The variety is in fact so great that there might be a danger of miscellaneity – if, that is, the energy of the writing didn't keep propelling the poem forward with such vigour that the reader never has time to question where – if anywhere – the work might be headed, or how – or whether – it might achieve unity. ('You never know which moment will be your next.') However, any sense of miscellaneity fades as the architecture of the triptych becomes plain on arrival at its second panel, about

Ridgewood, and then at its third panel, about Glendale, where in each case the sequence of forms is identical to that in the Greenpoint panel.

The work thus consists of three parallel series of different poetic forms, in which individual poems address widely varied subject matter with varying degrees of subjectivity, each poem contributing to the articulation of a different facet of the poet's perception of a particular neighbourhood, while at the same time participating in and being contained by the overarching structure of the poem. This architectural coherence governing the work as a whole does not, however, dilute the particularity of any part of it, and in this way the poem can be seen as being similar to a cubist painting. The poem's formal juxtapositions and patternings create in a time-bound medium an equivalent of the spatial practice, as Hubbell describes it, of 'the Cubist painter ... showing the object from many directions, and in many spatial relationships'. Comparing the work of Gertrude Stein with that of Picasso, Hubbell states: 'as the Cubist painter took an object apart and then reassembled the parts according to a completely autonomous sense of design, so she disintegrated her ideational content and reorganized it into a purely formal design' ('Stein: First Period', 194). In Hubbell's triptych the neighbourhoods of Long Island have been taken apart and the resulting multiple viewpoints have been reorganised into the 'purely formal design' of the poem – a design so strong that it allows a huge variety of matter to enter the poem and be contained there without any item either losing its own quiddity or disrupting the architectural structure of the whole work.[5]

Mid-length modernist poems have taken various forms: spikily discontinuous sequences (*Hugh Selwyn Mauberley*), structures shaped by a sonata-like musical architecture (*The Waste Land*, Basil Bunting's various 'Sonatas'), or even just a fluently Byronic talkativeness (W. H. Auden's 'Letter to Lord Byron'). *Long Island Triptych* follows none of these models. More in the tradition of Stein than of any of the poets just mentioned, it is the product of considerable traditional formal expertise deployed in the service of a cubist imagination, and as such does not – as far as I know – resemble any other twentieth-century mid-length poem.

Except, perhaps, Hubbell's own second attempt at a similarly structured poem, *Atlantic Triptych*. This had a much longer gestation than the earlier triptych. The inner flap of the dust jacket of *Double*

Triptych (1974), which prints the two poems together, tells us that while the Long Island poem was written in 1945 and published in 1947, *Atlantic Triptych* was begun in Hartford in 1950, finished in Kyoto in 1964, and was first published by Ikuta Press in Kobe in 1971.

As the title suggests, the second triptych has a wider geographical reach: the Atlantic rather than just one island at that ocean's edge. There are gains from this shift in scale: the first poem of each panel is a hymn to the ocean and the myriad forms of life inhabiting its depths and shallows: sea-cucumbers, lilies, shrimps with long legs, glass sponges, the enormous monocanthus, broad-leaved sargassum, kelp, red algae, diatoms, dinoflagellates, coccolithophoridae, pipe fish and needle fish – to list only some of the marine flora and fauna catalogued in the very first poem of the book. However, this scaling-up also has disadvantages: while each panel of the first triptych benefitted from being firmly grounded in a particular, inhabited place, one whose history is narrated in the second poem of each panel and whose name provides the title of the panel, in *Atlantic Triptych* the panels are titled simply 'Part One', 'Part Two', and 'Part Three', and there is no attempt to anchor the poem in a specific locality and its history. History is in fact narrated in the poems that appear as Part V of each of the three panels, but this history is far-flung and various, and, in the absence of a sense of local inhabitation of the kind seen in the first triptych, it's not entirely clear why the military, linguistic and ecclesiastical histories of Poland, Ruthenia or Silesia are being recounted in such detail. The histories included in the poem are so disparate and so widely distributed geographically and culturally that it seems virtually impossible for these 'multiple perceptions from discrete points of view' to be expressed in 'a single composite shape' – to use Edward F. Fry's words referring to the work of Cézanne (37). As a result the poem, for all its parallel structuring does not hang together quite so well as a unified and aesthetically satisfying shape as the earlier work did.

A related feature that tends to weaken the unity of the second triptych is the lack of any strongly autobiographical element. In the earlier triptych, poems of personal experience are interspersed among poems concerning locality, history, or philosophy, a mingling which further helps to ground the poem as a whole in a sense of lived experience: we have the feeling that we are in the presence of an astute, complex, interested, and variously engaged mind interacting with a many-faceted environment. This presence of an 'I', whether that presence is explicitly signalled by the first-person pronoun or is merely implied, creates the sense that there is an invisible magnetic or gravitational field holding the universe of the poem together as entity and system. Stenographers, delicatessens, the Canarsie Indians, Mae West, the great institution of the human heart, Vivekananda, the ancient inhabitants of Germany, gold from Wicklow, Brancusi's bird, and 'the loud bullshitting in the pool rooms and the bowling alleys' of Greenpoint, all of which appear in the first panel of *Long Island Triptych*, are certainly various enough – and each as important as another, as Stein claimed both details and brush strokes should be ('Transatlantic Interview', 15) – but they are held in a multi-faceted unity not only by the overarching poetic form but by the sense that they are all equally facets of the curiosity, knowledge, and perceptions of an inhabitant of the place named in the poem's title. This is not the case in quite the same way in *Atlantic Triptych*.

There are marvellous moments in the second triptych, however. The hymns to the ocean that open each part have already been mentioned, and Part VIII of each panel is short and strong, each piece powerfully expressive of the speaker's despair at the irredeemable cruelty and de-structiveness of the human race – a dark and frequently recurring motif in the poem. Not all is darkness in *Atlantic Triptych*, however, and perhaps the single most enjoyable piece is the eighth poem of 'Part One', which consists of nine sprightly *terza rima* poems describing the work and narrating the life-stories – from Alcman and Sappho to Pindar and Bachyllides – of the canonical Nine Lyric Poets of ancient Greece as defined by the scholars of Hellenistic Alexandria. This is literary history insouciantly carried out in a demanding verse form, each poet accurately and wittily described both as person and as poet, and judiciously placed in a historical narrative running from Alcman's 'Aeolian grace and Ionian wit' through to the Old Comedy, where the human mind 'went down swinging' with 'its last word … a shout.'

THE HARTFORD POEMS

In 1946 Hubbell left New York to teach the history of drama at the Randall School in Hartford, Connecticut, and stayed there until 1953, when he departed for Japan; in a letter to Yoko Danno he says that while in Hartford 'I had my most prolific time and I think my best' ('Letters', 17-18). Forty-seven poems from this period were eventually gathered as Part One of *Seventy Poems*, published by Alan Swallow in 1965. (The twenty-three poems included in the second part of the book are products of his first decade in Japan.) None of the Hartford poems are anything like as ambitious as the two triptychs, but many of them, even if on a smaller scale, are more focused and successful than the second of the two long poems. *Seventy Poems* is very various in subject matter and tone. Some kinds of poem that had previously appeared in Hubbell's work – sonnets or rhymed lyrics of baffled desire, for example – are gone for good: none appear in this new book, nor will any appear in his later work.[6] But among the considerable variety in the collection there are some loose groups of poems that are developments – or even finalisations – of previous thematic initiatives, and some which represent emerging concerns that will only get stronger in his later books.

The first of these groups of poems is concerned with geology and the most ancient fossil evidences of life, and in particular with a search for the origins of art in both pre-human history and the early history of *Homo sapiens*. The first and longest poem of this group, 'The First Architect', concerns the creative activities of the diatom, an organism defined by *Merriam-Webster* as 'any of a class … of minute planktonic unicellular or colonial algae with silicified skeletons'. Diatoms are so small as to be invisible to the human eye, but if viewed under a microscope, it is possible to see that their valves are 'sculptured', and that their 'convex walls of silica' consist of two shells

> Which fit each other neatly as a pill box
> Fits the pill box cover [and] are wrought
> With no less concentration
> Than the Apollonian pediment at Olympia.[7]

This, Hubbell claims, must be a 'conscious shaping' since 'no two [are] alike.' Further, he goes on to claim that we are still

> After a billion years of biological evolution,
> Doing the same thing. We are consciously

Making forms. Making form.
An invisible plant making its invisible house

– and that if László Moholy-Nagy were similarly examined under
a microscope, he 'would be seen doing the same thing.' I'm not sure
that a single diatom can be seen as a 'conscious' shaper of forms in the
way that Moholy-Nagy can, but I think Hubbell's point here is that the
creation of forms – no two of which are alike – is the outcome of a basic,
exuberant, and inexpungible urge of the life force, and that it is in this
urge that art has its origins. The poem thus ends: 'An invisible plant
making its invisible house, / Are where you have to begin if you want to
understand / Art.' This idea, and this poem, were important enough to
Hubbell for him to reprint the poem as the title poem of his last book in
1984, where he also included 'The Birth of the Diatom: A Nativity Play',
a skit originally published in a small-press pamphlet by the Banyan Press
in 1949; it includes the delightfully self-deprecating lines:

> *First Diatom*
> I am no ordinary alga.
> I am an artist.
> The basso rilievo where my valves are joined
> Has been compared
> To the Apollonian pediment at Olympia.
>
> *Second Diatom*
> My God, she's been reading Hubbell.

The next poem in this group does not make any such claims, but is rather
a song of praise for the 'Ordovician Fossil Algae' of the poem's title. In
the first edition of *Seventy Poems*, on the page facing the poem, there is
a photograph from the American Museum of Natural History of a rock
printed with fossilised ferns (*Pecopteris denata*); this, Hubbell claims, 'is
the oldest book / That I can read with pleasure'. The poem finishes:

> This rock is my favorite book, my favorite picture,
> My dependable scripture,
> My sense of wholeness, a billion years at my elbow.

The next poem, 'Coutchiching Schist', is about 'the oldest rock / in North America' created when 'Earth's burden / of life was new / that now sticks / in her maw' – these last four lines showing signs of a prescient concern about the ongoing destruction of planet Earth by the human species, a disquiet that will grow more prominent in later poems. 'Foraminifer' marks a slight return to the theme of 'The First Architect' as the ameboid of the title – 'this exquisite, just visible architect' – is described as secreting 'a hard calcerous shell' before dying 'in rain upon the ocean floor / One third of which is paved / With foraminifer's abandoned house.' 'The Courtship of the Annelida' returns to the theme of the origins of art, seeing the mating dance of segmented worms as being the point of origin of the rites of Osiris and Dionysus, activities which later blossomed into the drama of Shakespeare and Shaw.

This cluster of loosely associated pieces culminates in a pair of poems about modernist masters in the visual arts, tributes to Malevich and Mondrian (with black and white illustrations of work by both artists printed in the book). Malevich is seen as 'entirely artist', as someone whose 'circle and … square are impregnable', while Mondrian is a 'mathematician and saint' whose 'pure canvases' make it perfectly clear that 'it is no longer necessary / For a serious man to renounce art.' These two poems complement his pieces in earlier books in praise of Brancusi and Duchamp. All four artists are mentioned in a single sentence of 'Autobiography in Fifty Sentences' (1971) as being all he remembers from his twenty years in New York, and Brancusi appears in the poem 'Pebbles', published in *The First Architect* (1982) – where it is claimed that only he could have made something as beautiful as the two pebbles from the beach at Miho no Matsubara, 'so marvelously shaped / by the immemorial sculpture of the ocean', which are now lying on Hubbell's desk. Other than these two instances, however, none of these artists appear in Hubbell's books published in Japan. He continued to speak about them and their importance to him, but there are no more poems directly focused on them and their work; perhaps he felt that by this stage he had said what he had to say.

There is also a small group of poems from the post-Hiroshima age – 'Secret Weapon', 'Ant Hill', and 'After', the last of these presenting a haunting picture of the post-human planet (although the poem doesn't specify whether humans have disappeared from the face of the earth as a result of nuclear or ecological catastrophe). There are satires ('Sapphics on an Ashtray in the Shape of a Piano') and light verse ('Half Century') – carried off with great formal adroitness in both cases. There are also several poems about dreams and identity, including the powerful 'Dreams', which asks whether the figures that 'inhabit my changing dreams' are

> … indeed projections of my importance,
> Or am I rather a collection, held loosely together,
> Of shaken leaves, of easily broken stems,
> And you the enormous root?

The metaphor of a tree here points to Hubbell's increasing concern with nature in the form both of trees (considered figuratively and as living beings in their own right) and of creatures of various kinds noticed in all their particularity. An elegy for a blown-down tree, 'Blue Spruce' – 'in death no less mysterious than a man, / Its whereabouts unknown' – had already appeared in *Long Island Triptych and Other Poems*, and in Part One of *Seventy Poems* there are two other poems ('Tree' and 'Canadian Spruce') in which a tree is the central character and is seen as deserving of attention and respect as a living thing. In addition, in both parts of *Seventy Poems* there are many poems describing living creatures in compassionate and empathetic ways. In poems of this type, there is usually an attempt to see things from the creature's point of view or else to find unexpected pleasure or beauty in a creature which we are inclined to be repulsed by ('Alligator Song' and 'Python' are examples in Part One). This sympathic approach to the creaturely is even more noticeable in Part Two of the same book, set in Japan, and it becomes yet more prominent in *Walking Through Namba* (1978), which includes no fewer than eighteen poems about creatures reprinted from the two parts of *Seventy Poems* – half of them from the Hartford era – to accompany more recent poems on the same theme. The later book also includes the three poems about trees mentioned above, together with poems about tropical fish, insects, and cats reprinted from *Winter-Burning*. It seems as if in some of the poems written in Hartford Hubbell was laying down and establishing themes and motifs that would continue to engage him in his later work, and that when he included so many previously published poems in *Walking Through Namba* – only sixteen of the forty poems in the book were new – he was recasting his canon in such a way as to represent a new and important emphasis in his poetry. Considering that these poems were written between 1945 and 1978, their ecological and animal-centred approach seems prescient.

WALKING LIGHTLY

On 6 October 1953 Hubbell arrived by ship in Japan, thus beginning the last major stage of his life story. He recorded his feelings about this occasion in 'In Yokohama Harbor', the poem which opens Part Two of *Seventy Poems*:

> What am I doing here,
> where my people unleashed
> the age of horror
>
> sowing the plague
> that will kill us all?
> Can I be loved?
>
> Is it possible
> this earth will not scorch
> the soles of my feet?
>
> Lord Buddha and Lord Christ
> help me to walk
> lightly on this soil.

Given that it had only been eight years since the obliteration of Hiroshima and Nagasaki, and only eighteen months since the end of the American Occupation of Japan, Hubbell's trepidation is understandable. In the end, though, there was no need for worry: he did indeed walk lightly on the soil of Japan, and, judging by the actions and statements of his Japanese friends, colleagues and students over the next thirty or forty years, the answer to the question 'Can I be loved?' was in the affirmative.

Although he hadn't originally intended to go to Japan, let alone settle there, once he arrived, it suited him so well that he never left again, naturalising as a Japanese citizen in 1960.

Even if Japan had not been his first thought as a destination – Italy had been his original plan – he was certainly ready to leave America. There were worries about job security in Hartford, and, as Donald Richie says, he was beginning to despair of American poetry (Richie, 7). Kanaseki Hisao reports that Hubbell himself put it more forcefully when much later he explained why he had never returned to the United States: 'The reason he gave was that in that country the rich people hold complete sway and artists and poets were totally neglected by society; he had no use for such a country.' (Kanaseki, 49-50). Hubbell's sentiments are even more forcefully expressed in his uncollected poem 'Leaving Honolulu', which appears in his posthumously published *Travel Diary 1953–1954* immediately before the already quoted 'In Yokohama Harbor'. It begins, 'As I leave American soil / I have this to say to my countrymen', and it ends:

> You are the richest people in the world
> And the luckiest.
>
> From anyone else I could take
> Prejudice and ignorance and vulgarity
>
> But not from you,
> You pursy bastards. Aloha.

I'm not sure if this counts as a poem – even if the force of its plain-speaking was likely highly therapeutic. Presumably Hubbell also had his doubts on this score as neither this poem nor any of the other poems set in America from the time he shook the dust of Hartford off his shoes (his own phrase) to his departure from Hawaii were ever published, while a number of those in the rest of the diary, from Yokohama onwards, appeared in order of composition in Part Two of *Seventy Poems*.

He narrated the chain of events that led him, without having initially intended it, to Japan when Yoko Danno interviewed him in 1994:

In Osaka Ichidai [City College], the German Department got

a German to come to Japan for two years to teach and the English Department was jealous, so the head of the English Department wanted to have a foreigner for his department, and Kanaseki Hisao was in that department, and he said to Hisao, 'You know a lot of foreigners, so recommend somebody.'[8] So he asked Mrs. Ruth Fuller Sasaki and she recommended me. ('Interview', 60)

Ruth Fuller Sasaki (1892–1967) was an American Buddhist, who played a leading role in the development of Buddhism in America, and who after 1949 lived mostly in Kyoto, where in 1957 she founded the First Zen Institute of America in Japan with the aim of translating into English important classics of the Zen Buddhist canon.[9] Kanaseki Hisao at the time of Hubbell's arrival was a young scholar; he later became known as a leading Japanese authority on modern American and Native American poetry.

Hubbell accepted the job offer made by Osaka Ichidai, but then the university administration decided not to fund the position, so Sasaki had to write to Hubbell to say that the job offer had been withdrawn. At just about the same time, Hubbell received from a cousin a legacy of $9,000 – a considerable sum at that time – so when he saw Sasaki during her next visit to New York in May 1953, he told her that he felt 'very embarrassed' as he had told everyone that he was going to Japan; he also said that as a result of the inheritance, he could pay his own way there.

I said, 'Do you think if I go there I could get a job?' and she said, 'If you come, I will give you a job.' So I came and she gave me a job: cataloguing the works in her library. ('Interview', 61)

So, Hubbell arrived in Japan on 6 October and shortly thereafter went to Kyoto, where he had dinner with Sasaki and Kanaseki; the latter invited Hubbell to lunch to meet Ueno Naozō, the president of the prestigious Dōshisha University, who then invited Hubbell to give a lecture at the university's Shakespeare festival in November; Hubbell did this, and after the lecture was offered a professorship. In a later poem, 'At Kanryuji' written after his retirement from Dōshisha and move to Kobe, Hubbell wrote of his escape as a young man from Hartford to New York 'and from thence / to Kyoto / and finally to Kobe'

and I said to myself:
There is something
that is taking care of me.

It did indeed seem that, after the stormy passages of the 1930s and
1940s, things began – and continued – to go well for him from the time
of his arrival in Japan onwards. As he put it in 'Rough Crossing', the
final poem in his pamphlet *Autobiography* (1971), 'I always knew that
there was land ahead, / And now I have crossed.'

STAYING STILL, THEN MOVING

Although Hubbell claimed that he had never dreamed of going to Japan,
he was in many ways well prepared for residence there: he was well-
versed both in the Buddhist tradition and in Japanese literature. He had
always been deeply interested in Asian religions: in 'There's One Born
Every Minute', an uncollected autobiographical poem, he remembers
some key involvements of his adolescence: first Ibsen, then George
Borrow, and then 'religion comes up like thunder / Ramacharaka,
Blavatsky, Vivekananda'. Further, the poem 'The Road Not Taken' in
Climbing to Monfumo (1971) shows, in its record of a head-on encounter
with a Buddhist text at the age of sixteen, how seriously he took this
involvement. When, seventy-seven years after the moment of choice
described in that poem, Yoko Danno asked him who, in his opinion,
were 'the five greatest human beings who have ever lived,' the Buddha
was at the top of a list that included Nagarjuna, Shankaracharya, Lao-
Tsu, and Mahavira, between them representing the major Asian religions
of Buddhism, Hinduism, Taoism, and Jainism; the Buddha was also first
on the list of five persons, past or present, who had most influenced
him, ahead of Shakespeare, Ibsen, Eleanora Duse, and his aunt Laura
Williams ('Interview', 64-65). At the time that Donald Richie met him
in 1943, Hubbell was already attending the evening meetings of Ruth
Fuller Sasaki's First Zen Institute of America in New York, held in her
East Side town house (Richie, 6).

Having arrived in Japan, Hubbell took to his life there like a duck to
water: in 1994 he told Yoko Danno that he always felt more at home in

Japan than in America ('Interview', 58). However, Hubbell by no means abandoned his previous cultural involvements – Shakespeare, Beethoven, Brancusi – but, in addition to his engagement with Buddhism, there were, as Yoko Danno points out in her afterword to this volume, three other main religious or cultural focuses specific to his life in Japan: Shinto, nō theatre, and Japanese pop music. In her memoir of Hubbell, Yoko Danno writes of his fascination with the rituals, music and dance of Shinto ceremonies, such as the annual ceremony at the Kamogamo shrine in Kyoto or the big annual festival of Kasuga in Nara. She also reports that when in his final days he was in an uncomfortable open hospital ward, Ueno Hisako 'obtained for him a private room in a Christian hospital, but he refused to move into it, saying he was dedicated to Shinto, not to Christianity.'

Hubbell's response to nō drama, which he first experienced on 21 October 1953 at the Kongō Nōgaku-dō [Kongō Nō Theatre] in Kyoto, was immediate, total and ever after unwavering. In his 'Notes on Nō' in *Second Miscellany*, published by Ikuta Press in 1975, he quotes Rimbaud's statement 'Action is a way of spoiling something,' and then adds that 'this might have been said by a Japanese. Action in Japanese art, like the visible portion of an iceberg, is no more than one eighth of the total mass. This is seen most clearly, perhaps, in Nō dancing.' He then elaborates:

> In the West a dancer is always moving. If he stopped moving the audience would consider that he had stopped dancing. But in the Nō the dancer can stand still for minutes at a time, then when he does move there is a center of intensity from which his movement can derive impact and significance. This is seen best, I think, in the great dance in the first act of *Dōjōji*. The *shite* [leading actor] stands motionless for many minutes, while the *tsutsumi* [hip drum] player howls and taps out the exacerbating rhythms of this marvelous and intricate score. Suddenly the *shite* slightly moves one foot. This slight movement of the foot is terrifying. But it is the long awful moments of stillness before the movement that produce the nervous shudder when the foot moves. This intensity is greater than could be achieved by all the leaps and writhings in the repertory of the occidental dancer. (*Second Miscellany*, 23)

This, I think, captures the essence of nō very well; the only parallel I can think of is that part of Philip Whalen's 'Birthday Poem' that describes a Kyoto performance of the same play, *Dōjōji,* and focuses in the same way on the movement of the foot and the stillness before and after it: 'Each motion followed by unendurable stillness and silence' (Whalen, 46-47). Given Hubbell's previous aesthetic commitments, it's easy to understand why he loved this form of theatre: it could almost be described as a living marriage of Shakespearean performance with the austerity of artists such as Malevich and Mondrian; in Rand Castile's opinion, 'the prescribed movements of the nō, the spareness, the dignity of the form, the "finish" appealed to Lindley's sense of order and artistry' (Castile, 19). Castile goes on to say, 'It seemed to us that he was always boarding a train, going off to catch some play in another district, a play, perhaps, which he had not yet seen' (Castile, 19-20).

Or perhaps he was going off to catch a concert of Japanese pop music, a very different aesthetic from nō. Hubbell was a noted fan of Hashi Yukio, who had his first major hit in 1960 at the age of seventeen. Hashi sang *enka*, a modernised variation of a traditional Japanese song style, which became popular in the 1960s, partly in resistance to the influence of Elvis Presley and American pop music generally. Hashi was a major figure in the development of this 'modern *enka*' style and had a series of hits over a period of sixty years, only retiring in 2023 with a farewell concert on his eightieth birthday. According to Hatano Kazuko, a colleague at Mukogawa Women's University in Kobe, where Hubbell had his last teaching position, he was a member of Hashi's fan club, had his own reserved seat in the front row for Hashi's performances, travelled to Tokyo, Nagoya and Osaka for his annual concerts, and would often attend the same performance four or five times (Hatano, 26).

With aesthetic experiences ranging from *Dōjōji* to Hashi Yukio, Hubbell seems to have greatly enjoyed his life in Japan, and much of this pleasure is evident in Part Two of *Seventy Poems,* and in his last three books of poetry, all published by Yoko Danno's Ikuta Press in Kobe: *Climbing to Monfumo* (1977), *Walking Through Namba* (1978), and *The First Architect* (1982). This is not to say that all the poems in these three books are about Japan – there is a wide variety of topics, settings, forms, and styles – but the poems about Japan in all four books are notably genial and observant. These are often slight poems, to be sure, but the slightness, the lightness of touch, is deliberate and in the service – in a rather Zen-like way – of the valuing of the small, the particular, and the humane aspects of everyday experience.

As mentioned earlier, there is in *Walking Through Namba* a noticeable emphasis on nature, the environment, animals, and plants, and this concern is also evident in poems in the other late books; in addition there are poems directly addressing the planetary crisis brought on by human depredation. There are also poems directly about Japan, whether descriptions of places visited or of walks through city streets. There is also a touching and respectful poem 'For the Emperor's 77th Birthday', which focuses on the Emperor Hirohito's abiding interest in marine biology, and an elegy for Teshima-sensei, a leading nō actor (and Living National Treasure) who lived in the same Kyoto neighbourhood as Hubbell. Old themes reappear: 'Missa Solemnis', 'Neandertal', 'Bacteria', and 'Chiba-ken' are all concerned with the origins of art. Old places are revisited: Eleanora Duse's grave in the title poem of *Climbing to Monfumo*, and Puerto Rico in the poem of that title in the 1978 volume. There are skilful and witty epigrams and light verse; personal reflections; and powerful attacks on racism, human cruelty, and injustice – all of which Hubbell had long detested. The variety is impressive.

LAST WORDS

After Hubbell retired from Dōshisha University in Kyoto in 1970, he moved to Kobe to teach at Mukogawa Women's University until 1985; he then returned to live in Kyoto, where he died in hospital on 2 October 1994. He had a Shinto funeral performed by the priests of the Ōta Jinja – the shrine that was the sole beneficiary of his will (Richie, 8).

He had had a long and interesting life, one not without difficulties in the first, American, part of it, but it seems that he indeed found his proper place in the second half of his life. He clearly loved living in Japan, delighted in its culture, and had a great number of close friends in both Kyoto and Kobe. In return, he was much loved and respected by everybody, Japanese or foreign, who knew him, as the warmth of the portraits, comments, and anecdotes in the volume of tributes, *Autumn Stone in the Woods,* published three years after his death, makes clear – indeed, the mere fact of the existence of such a book speaks volumes. His mentorship of poet Yoko Danno, whose English-language writing he encouraged, and of translator Hiroaki Sato, whom he taught at Dōshisha, are important parts of his legacy – and perhaps the most complete tribute to him and his influence is that by Yoko Danno which appears as the afterword to this book.

Hubbell's writing career was as remarkable as his life, developing as it did through three distinct phases: first, the formal lyrics of his New York period, followed by his ambitious 1940s modernism, before arriving at his late style: light, small-scale, humorous, observant, respectful of the particular, and (mostly) genial. Yet, in spite of this stylistic odyssey, the voice in the poems is always recognisable as his own. There are also recognisable themes: Kanaseki Hisao reports Hubbell saying to him that 'if there were consistent themes in his poetry, they were probably adoration for things that were beautiful, be they of the natural world or manmade, and anger at humanity's endless cruelties' (Kanaseki, 51). There is also consistent spareness, focus and skill in the details of the writing, whether that writing is formal – ranging in scale from epigrammatic couplet to double sestina – or free verse. His early work is exquisitely done even if it perhaps remains to some extent caught in its era; his last work is attractive in its confidence, variousness and lightness; but my feeling is that it is the two central books in his oeuvre – *Long Island Triptych and Other Poems* and the first part of *Seventy Poems* – which together contain his work of the 1940s, that are his greatest achievement. My hope is that this *Selected Poems*, and this introduction, might help to restore his work to wider circulation.

Paul Rossiter
Tokyo, March 2025

NOTES

¹ The Stein-Hubbell correspondence has been preserved in the Beinecke Rare Book and Manuscript Library at Yale. According to Hubbell himself ('Interview', 62), this correspondence began when Hubbell wrote and published an article about her work that somebody showed to Stein, leading her to contact him. He did in fact write an article about her, but it was not published until much later ('The Plain Edition of Gertrude Stein' *Contempo*, Vol. III, No. 12, 25 October 1933); however, the correspondence from 1928 in the Yale archive supports the narrative given in the main text above. Hubbell's letter to Jolas: 15 November 1928, YCAL MSS 76, Box III f. 2261; Stein's note to Hubbell: 12 December 1928. YCAL MSS 77, Box 10 f. 128. Gertrude Stein and Alice B. Toklas Papers, Yale Collection of American Literature. Beinecke Rare Book and Manuscript Library.

² November 1932. YCAL MSS 76, Box III f. 2261. Gertrude Stein and Alice B. Toklas Papers, Yale Collection of American Literature. Beinecke Rare Book and Manuscript Library.

³ The San Juan mentioned here is the capital of Puerto Rico. Ueno (39) reports that Hubbell told her that in 1940 he took further time off from the library to spend six months living in Puerto Rico, again subsidised by a rich friend. This friend seems to have been William Alexander Percy, the editor of the Yale Younger Poets Series, who helped Hubbell with the manuscript of *Dark Pavilion* during the period 1925-1927 and then recommended him for the award (Wise, 209). In a 1940 letter to a friend Percy described how when he visited New York in that year, he found Hubbell 'on the edge of a breakdown' and so 'shipped him to Puerto Rico' (Wise, 329). As Hubbell and Percy were close friends and frequent correspondents from the 1920s to Percy's death in 1942, it's possible that it was also Percy who paid for Hubbell's trip to Italy in 1935.

⁴ This section of this introduction shares some paragraphs with the afterword to the separate Isobar Press edition of *Long Island Triptych*.

⁵ Unfortunately, exigencies of space prevent the printing of *Long Island Triptych* in full in this *Selected Poems*. The complete text may be found, however, in the separate Isobar Press edition of the poem published simultaneously with this volume, one which includes an afterword discussing the poem's architecture in greater depth and investigating the

ways in which this might have been influenced both by cubism and by Hubbell's engagement with the work of Gertrude Stein. Here, however, this architecture can only be outlined in an attempt to suggest its originality and its formal rigour. Hopefully, a sufficient number of poems from 'Greenpoint' (printed complete), 'Ridgewood' (the first five poems) and 'Glendale' (six poems from various points in the section) have been included in this *Selected Poems* to make the parallelism sufficiently (if not completely) visible.

6   In a letter written to David Burleigh in the 1980s, Hubbell said: 'I've always had a special interest in sonnets. My first few books contained lots of them, but now for many years I haven't been able to write them' ('One of the Few', 32).

7   In a lecture titled 'Origins of Art' given in November 1945 (a date which provides a *terminus ante quem* for the composition of the poem), Hubbell quoted the whole of 'The First Architect', and in introducing the poem commented that the diatom's shells 'are inconceivably delicate and are covered with what can only be described as abstract sculpture, in relief, of great beauty' (13).

8   Some background information may be useful here. In 1953 Japanese universities were beginning to get back on their feet after the catastrophe of the war, and the departments specialising in foreign languages and literatures were desperate to employ qualified teachers who were native speakers of those languages. In contrast to the twenty-first century, when there are many well-qualified foreign nationals living and teaching in Japan, in 1953 there was almost no one available, and any university that managed to employ a native-speaker teacher counted itself as fortunate indeed – hence the jealousy of the German Department on the part of the head of the English Department.

9   The members of the institute included major Japanese scholars of Chinese and, on the American side, the translators Philip Yampolsky and Burton Watson, and the poet Gary Snyder. Kanaseki Hisao was also a member.

BIBLIOGRAPHY

PRIMARY SOURCES

All quotations from Lindley Williams Hubbell are from: Hubbell, Lindley Williams. *The Works of Lindley Williams Hubbell*. Ed. Makoto Ozaki. CD-Rom edition. Kyoto: Iris Press, 2005.

The main source for biographical details is: Burleigh, David and Hiroaki Sato (eds.). *Autumn Stone in the Woods: A Tribute to Lindley Williams Hubbell*. Middletown Springs, VT: P. S., A Press, 1997. This book of tributes includes:

Burleigh, David. 'One of the Few.' 29–34.
Castile, Rand. 'Living in a Mondrian: Hubbell Telescopes
    the World.' 17–23.
Danno, Yoko. 'An Interview.' 57–65.
Hatano Kazuko. 'In Remembrance.' 25–27.
Kanaseki Hisao. 'The Last Modernist.' 49–52.
Richie, Donald. 'On First Meeting LWH.' 3–8.
Sato, Hiroaki. 'Autumn Stone in the Woods.' 9–16.
Ueno Hisako. 'The Man Who Hated Fakes.' 35–46.
Yamamoto Shigeki. 'List of Nō Dramas LWH Saw. 67–72.

OTHER WORKS

Blake, William. *Selected Poetry*. Ed. W. H. Stevenson. London: Penguin, 1988.

Burleigh, David. 'Defiant and Alone: The Poetry of Lindley Williams Hubbell.' *Ferris Studies*, 26 (1991): 167–78.

Gray, Richard. *American Poetry of the Twentieth Century*. Longman Literature in English Series. Harlow: Longman, 1990.

Hass, Robert, John Hollander, Carolyn Kizer, Nathaniel Mackey, and Marjorie Perloff (eds.). *American Poetry: The Twentieth Century, Volume Two: E. E. Cummings to May Swenson*. New York: Library of America, 2000.

Perkins, David. *A History of Modern Poetry: From the 1890s to the High Modernist Mode*. Cambridge, MA: Belknap, 1976.

Stein, Gertrude. 'Vacation in Brittany.' *The Little Review*, Vol. 8, No. 2 (Spring 1922): 5–6.

Stein, Gertrude. *Everybody's Autobiography*. New York: Random House, 1937.

Stein, Gertrude. 'A Transatlantic Interview, 1946'. In *A Primer for the Gradual Understanding of Gertrude Stein*. Ed. Robert Bartlett Haas. Los Angeles: Black Sparrow Press, 1971, 15–35.

Stevens, Wallace. *Collected Poetry and Prose*. Eds. Frank Kermode and Joan Richardson. New York: Library of America, 1997.

Whalen, Philip. *Severance Pay*. San Francisco: Four Seasons Foundation, 1970.

Wise, Benjamin E. *William Alexander Percy: The Curious Life of a Mississippi Planter and Sexual Freethinker*. Chapel Hill: University of North Carolina Press, 2012.

PART ONE

New York

Canada, Italy, Puerto Rico

Connecticut

1927–1953

from

DARK PAVILION (1927)

DARE TO BE LOST

Dare to be lost,
However bleak the cost;
Let your soul shelter no desire
Save to be pierced with steel and burned in fire.

Fear but this thing: that you should turn to rest
Safe but unblest;
Rather than suffer this,
Choose the abyss.
There is no soul that in this torment dies
Would have it otherwise.

REMEMBER THIS

Remember this, O pitiful heart:
As surely as lover and lover part,
So do a man and his sorrow take
Divergent paths, for healing's sake.

Remember this, O haunted mind:
The years are slow but certainly kind;
And every grief and every crime
Will seem less terrible, in time.

AD CASTITATEM

Now you are come – loosener of many girdles,
  Rifler of many zones,
Silent, terrible, guarding your secrets
  As the earth guards her bones.

You have brought night to my eyes and the year's end to my heart;
  The fruit on the twig unshaken
Is fed to worms; which, bleeding upon the ground,
  Might have been sweet if taken.

EPITAPH FOR A CHASTE YOUTH

My heart belonged, until I died,
To one I never lay beside.
I went through life distraught and haunted
By things unknown but not unwanted.

My flesh, that lay above my bones
As smooth as water-polished stones,
Gradually, as time was wasted,
Shrivelled like a fruit untasted.

Until at last, where all men mingle,
They laid me here, austere and single,
But scarcely minding it a bit,
Being by now inured to it.

WARNING

Because I loved the way the candle-light
Caressed your hair while someone played Ravel,
You need not think by that one tender sight
I shall be swept into the usual hell.
Because you have, as anyone can see,
Strength for your sire and beauty for your dam,
You need not look my way, you need not be
So insolently sure of what I am.

From your variety of autumn fires,
I fear you lack experience of ice
In delicate and many-colored spires
That lie not in your power to entice;
And there are reasons you were vain to seek
Why one may be a virgin – and a Greek.

SURRENDER

God, you will doubtless win me in the end.
When once too often I have seen great beauty
Rotting away, I shall remember duty
And turn to you as to an only friend.
Oh, I shall then be calm and wise and still,
And feel no more a sudden twinge of pain
At seeing clustered lilies in the rain,
Or one tall poplar naked on a hill.

I shall bow down where many knees have bent,
And you may mark my prayers until it sate you;
I shall be much too tired out to hate you;
After a little there will be content.
But do not dream, though I forget the rest,
That I could love you more than second best.

ADVICE

I could endure to have you die;
   Although I should be much bereft,
Still could I bear it, for I know
   There would be so much beauty left.
      But, if I might thus far make bold,
     I do forbid that you grow old.

Die if you must, for in the earth
   Your slow corruption would be hidden.
But to confront my strenuous eye
   With beauty's end, you are forbidden.
     So if you'd have me hold you dear,
     Do not survive your thirtieth year.

BIRTH-HOUR

There was rain falling as I walked through the quiet streets;
   It was still coming down, later, as I lay on the bed
Listening in the dark to the great drops striking the window;
   And I knew that something was born and something was dead.

My heart spoke to me out of the voices of the raindrops,
   Saying, 'From this night onward, until you are dead,
You will lie alone, you will lie without your desire;
   Not even in the grave will you find a colder bed.'

YOU WILL REMEMBER

You will remember all your life
   A night or two of stormy weather,
And maybe some of the things we said
   And most of the things we did together.
You will know how my city looks
   On a rainy night, when the sea-winds pelt –
But little enough of what I thought,
   And nothing at all of what I felt.

DARK PAVILION

It lies in ruins now, but it was always
   A terrible place to come upon at night;
And I have seen many and many a person,
   Confronted by it suddenly, take flight.

It was always a terrible place, but now that it lies in ruins,
   Nobody ever walks that way at all;
And mine are the only ears that ever listen
   When the bats knock and the rotten rafters fall.

from

THE TRACING OF A PORTAL (1931)

AFTERNOON FERRY

The rain fell slowly into the hushed city
  And into the dark water of the bay.
Gulls rode the tide on blocks of ice,
  Gray upon gray.

There was Hoboken ahead of me, and Union City,
  And the rain wetting my face,
And the boat plowing through water and broken ice
  From one desolate place to another desolate place.

UNDERTOW

Always at my feet,
Too plain to doubt,
I feel the pull of the tide
Dragging me out.

I strain to the shore, hearing
The receding foam hiss;
But the undertow is stronger.
I am no match for this.

In spite of all I can do
The water will rise
Over the knees and the heart,
Over the mouth and the eyes.

WANT

They sleep securely who lie down at night
    To share one bed with want.
A narrow sheet suffices to make room
    For this cold celebrant.

Night after night, in desperate city rooms
    Or on disheveled farms,
Straight in their chilly beds they turn to sleep
    With famine in their arms.

NEW YORK

The city rises from the sea like an iron lily.
    The city opens to the light like a cluster of metal flowers, rigid on
        the stem.
As a pool is fragrant with water lilies, so has the ocean brought forth
    Flowers without essence to pierce the air like blades.

For miles around the islands shed cold luster upon the waves,
    And in the center, like a flower or a gem harder than a flower,
The great lily, the lily of marble and steel
    Cutting the air with its petals.

Surely the heart is made whole that has beheld,
Perfect upon the stem, this flower.

A LETTER TO GERTRUDE STEIN

The roots have struck deep: tree root and flower root and the small
      absurd weed nourished by dust;
In this rich soil a whole generation that would have found death in
      the wind and the black ice,
But the roots were fast, the loam was packed tightly about them,
      the serried stalks were secure,
The earth was stronger than the deep ice, the earth gave back
      laughter to the laughter of the wind, the ice cracked.

In the cities it was the same: people leaned out of windows and
      sniffed the air and laughed,
Children flew past in a clatter of roller skates, children screamed,
      their voices louder than the clatter of their skates,
The older ones played ball in the streets, chairs were brought out
      on the pavements, women rocked back and forth,
In all the cities it was like this, and in the little towns no one stayed
      in the houses when work was done.

The miracle was this: that a man could look at his friend and say
      without shame,
'It is better to be dead than to laugh at a perfectly simple thing. To
      do that is worse than death.'
The miracle was that sweetness was not gone out of the sap, that
      the stem was not ashamed to bear blossoms,
That the roots were glad of the rain, that the slow wind was
      permitted gladly, that the boughs were fed willingly.

Love, the bright flower, and homage, the proud spearhead of the
      tall flower,
And laughter, a spike of mullein, whatever is simple and without
      harm, whatever is unashamed of the dust it wears on its leaves,
And the sanity of the grass, the wide cool sanity of the grass that asks
      one inch, two inches of earth, and one inch, two inches of air,
These shall be plaited into a sign to be given from hand to hand as
      a token and a remembrance.

LINE

I would take all color,
Watch it grow paler, duller;
I would see it fade from the stem, and see it die
Out of the morning sky and the evening sky.
I would have the intricate curve
Bent straight.
I have come to hate
All vehemence, the coarse tint and the fine.
I would see all beauty in a naked line.

THE DEAD

They are gone and not one of them went willingly;
  But the strongest will, no less than the weak, was broken,
The hand that clutched at the ledge was stricken loose,
  And the last word hushed while it was being spoken.

Not one of them went willingly, never a one
  But clutched at familiar objects to the last.
The reluctant, desperate fingers were slow to loosen;
  But not one held tightly enough, not one held fast.

THERE WILL BE NO ONE

There will be no one to tell them what I was like
  When youth was upon me and the pride of youth.
They will look at me with cold, incurious eyes;
  And there will be no one left to tell them the truth.

I shall be like a tree bearing winter in its veins,
  The trunk and the knotted boughs thereof being dead.
And there will be no one, there will be no one at all
  To tell them that a flowering branch once grew in its stead.

LAST SONG

This is the last,
Now it is over.
From friend and lover
I shall keep fast

The battered door;
Neither god nor mortal
The beleaguered portal
Shall enter more.

Bring riot and shout,
Bring swordsman and lancer;
You will have no answer,
The torches are out.

from

WINTER-BURNING (1938)

THE NINTH PLANET

Neither the evening star nor the morning star
  Will you ever be.
Lovers will never lift their eyes to you,
  Nor mariners at sea.

Be then the planet of the dispossessed
  Whose beacon never shone
Securely in the green light of evening,
  The orange light of dawn.

SONG

He that has died
And come to life once more
Has put away his pride
No less than his pain.
What was loved before
Will be loved again.

He that has lain
Recently in prison
Looks with a narrow eye
On the rounded sky,
But only for a season.
What was loved before
Will be loved again.

SONNET

The air is dark with arrows, the great hull
Burns level with the shore, hot in the eyes
Is blowing the contentious dust. Arise,
O terrible army of the beautiful,
Take in your naked hands the thunderous maces,
And javelins that slit the very bone,
But raise no banners more than nature's own
Painted upon your perishable faces.

Harry the land like Scythians, pour salt
In the wide furrows that your spears have ploughed,
That not again will propagate the proud
And poisonous weeds composted with our fault,
Nor that small, sorry plant that has of late
Abounded here, the narrow leaf of hate.

MASK

In early and in middle youth
The images are still confused
And shifting that eventually
Into individual truth
Harden, or are quite refused.

Soon the elect and single image,
Haphazardly and for no reason
Beyond the crotchet of a season
Chosen, will eclipse the sky
With its accidental plumage.

SONG

Seek fellowship of this
Gem, this whetted knife.
Scorn the hypothesis
Of inorganic life.

Seek further at the core
Than engine ever went,
Where sleeps the patient ore,
The rustless element.

THE THREE WISE MEN

Spirit and matter,
Said the dualist,
Are neatly placed
Like two pears on a platter.

You will find, said the monist,
Nothing there
But the nature of pear,
If you are honest.

Ha, said the zany,
A child could see
The answer will be
Neither one nor many.

THIS RICH CONTINENT

This rich continent, sombre with mosses hanging
From wrinkled boughs, where red and green macaws,
Raucous but healthy, sing in the warm air,
Where rush below, feeding the giant roots
The great waters, where deep in the sunken veins
    The ruby in the rock

Burns forever, all this oppresses the heart,
The narrow lungs and the thinned arteries
Find it immoderate and in excess,
Languor possesses the legs, the fingers drop
To the tuckered sides, and the eyes widen with horror
    At the multitudinous teeming.

So they have taken to islands for their being,
A green pinch in a crinkly sea, a neat
Tree topped with a tuft, and a tiny cove
Cut like a coin in the impeccable coast;
Here is a kingdom that a man may rule,
    Within an hour's brisk walk.

The islands are curtained with fog, but through the fissures
Desperate forays go forth in rickety dugouts,
Venomous barbs blown from the pursy mouths.
As for the mainland, that is a long time since
Forgotten and out of mind. See, the slick pennant
    Slaps at the spindling mast.

AIR PARADE

They flew in V's, like wild geese flying south,
Over the city to the river's mouth,

Over the harbor to the Jersey shore,
And still they came, and there were always more.

Their wings were spread like ganders, and their call
Was louder far but no less beautiful.

Their shadow swept the city like a cloud,
Darker and darker, till I cried aloud:

The beauty of one airplane in the sky
Is vehement enough for such as I.

HENRIK IBSEN

Seal the lips, that was always his way; beauty is no flower,
Beauty is a peak of ice, blue against bluer sky.
The word is implicit, not spoken; let it be secret,
A fox at the entrails, the cloak held tightly and no cry uttered.

The winged horse was shot under him, or so he said;
But the mountain peaks shine clear in the blue morning
And beauty is not a word to be bandied about.
The mouth drawn tight as a thread and the gimlet eyes knew what
      they knew.

The air cuts like a knife higher up; it is hard going.
For a moment they stood at the top with clouds under their feet;
But a slide of snow or the head's own dizziness brought them down,
And the clouds closed quietly over them. Nothing was altered.

And Emilie came that summer at Gossensass, before the leaves
Had begun to fall from the wooded slope of the valley;
And in the autumn a photograph saying in a crabbèd script:
An die Maisonne eines Septemberlebens.

And somewhat more: the nerves laid bare like a chart, the mind
Filed to a point, the heart cleansed; Helena,
The fingers caught in her hair; and at the hill's crest
Two women and a dead man, and the snow falling.

This is the city where men sleep
With their backs against the walls of warehouses;
Where old women, down at the heels
And draggle skirted, weep,
Throwing stale meat to cats.

This is the city where old men in the evening
Shuffle home to furnished rooms,
And lie down stark,
Their eyes agape in the darkness,
Facing their threadbare dooms.

And here I stood, one winter afternoon,
Startled, arrested, seeing face to face
Brancusi's golden bird.
The city roared about me, but I heard
Only the bird singing.

from **THREE LETTERS**

I

To Cleon, chaire:
I am sorry the fever kept you from Olympia.
Telesicrates won the wrestling, Hagesias' mules
Were swiftest, Aristomenes of Aegina,
The youngest son of old Diagoras,
Running the terrible foot race in full armor,
Broke the world's record and fell straightway dead,
Thus honoring the gods and his father's name.

But maybe you didn't intend to go this year;
You that are always sticking your long nose
Into the isms of our crack-pot age.
As for the gods, they don't exist at all.
It is Leukippos who favors us with this,
Erecting in their stead (on his own say so)
A small inscrutable thing he calls an atom.
This is, I gather, smaller than a gnat,
Or a gnat's egg, or whatever else is smaller,
But joined together (they are quite numerous)
They make the olive groves of Cythera,
Arcesilas the son of Megacles,
And whatsoever else is noble or fair.
This strikes me as somewhat less than sensible.
It's true I've not seen Phoebus, but I suspect
It's just as true he's never seen an atom
(And if I could see one thing or the other,
I'd rather see Apollo string his bow
Than twenty million atoms copulating.)
For great effects I look for noble causes,
And so, with imperfections here and there,
The world being lovely, beyond controversy,
I think the burden of proof lies flat on him.

Perhaps you don't like Leukippos more than I do,
Being deep in the wisdom of Pythagoras:
A holy man, I'm sure, but somewhat addled.
Never, the longest day I hope to live,
Shall I forget Jason, the Pythagorean,
Standing up naked in the gymnasium,
His round abdomen shining like the moon,
Shouting at the boy who scraped the unguent from him,
'Never eat beans, if you would save your soul!'
And now Tryphaena (surely you remember her?)
Fancies herself a latter-day Theano.
I saw her last night at Alcimedon's dinner.
Tryphaena was a hot piece in her day,
But now, her breasts being fallen and her throat
No longer worthy of Praxiteles,
She is occupied with other things perforce.
Last night, when a slice of boar was laid before her,
She fell to blubbering in the chestnut sauce,
Saying, 'Who knows but this defenceless creature,
So foully slaughtered for our appetite,
May well have been my grandmother who died
A year ago last Thesmophoria.'
Well, women are good for one thing anyway.

Or have you joined the Orphic society
That meets on the full moon at Euphorion's,
Where they engage to purge themselves entire
Of the five senses' taint, winning release
From the envious circle of birth and death and birth?
Their doctrines are complicated, but they fail
To explain why anyone should want release
From sweet familiar comforts of the flesh
Which, taken in excess, are poison surely,
But used in moderation, as is seemly,
Are all we know of good and fair and true.

Oh, Cleon, Cleon, as you came head foremost
Into the world, go headfirst out of it,
Lest you be born a goose next time.
                              Farewell.

II

To Marcus, greeting:
I missed you at the Coliseum yesterday.
Up to your neck in books? Sulpicia tells me
You have usurped upon your narrow shoulders
The burden that was laid on Atlas once.
Pray leave it there; he is accustomed to it.
All your great thinkers contradict each other
And themselves; each one is right and the others crazy;
And you in the middle, spinning like a top.
The choice of gods is just as complicated.
New gods from the east are dumped upon our wharves
Like unfamiliar animals for the theatre.
Even Antinous has become a god;
The pretty boy from Bithynia that great Hadrian
Used for a mattress is a god, to whom
The reverend senators and grave aediles burn
A pinch of incense, laughing in their togas.
But there are lots worse than Antinous.
He lived, at least. Most are apocryphal.
Have you by any chance become a Christian?
The Christians multiply like rabbits lately
In spite of the prohibition of the law,
Though I must say, in simple fairness to them,
I have detected them in no worse crime
Than giving indigestion to our lions.
But that's not all: from Egypt, Lydia, Persia,

From India even (wherever on earth that is)
The gods come daily. Have you seen the new Diana,
With more teats than a sow, on the Aventine?
Ah, Marcus, Marcus, there was a time long since
When these august and venerated hills
Were saved in deadly peril from the Gauls
By the devoted cackling of our geese.
This is not likely to occur again.

If you must cram your sharp, exacting mind
Into a casket sealed with ambergris
And 'do not open' stamped upon the seal,
Need you so fast forget our master Zeno?
Who said (unless I'm wrong) no more than this:
Be kind to all, and take it on the chin.

But to return to more engrossing matters:
I missed you yesterday at the Coliseum,
And you missed something more: fifty young huskies,
Fresh from the gladiatorial college, made mincemeat
Of each other and themselves, and, in the finals,
The brand new giant from Cappadocia
(Imported at considerable expense)
Took on the young Andronicus. Rome's favorite.
I'm sorry to say he split him quite in two.
The youngster was clever at feinting with the sword
But the Cappadocian's a devil with the net.
This was the Andronicus that lay much, of late,
With our divine Empress (the whore) who bade him
Return unflecked and shining to her arms.
I think she will choose another man tonight.

OLD BOOKS

Sappho's dark hyacinth,
Prospero with his rod,
Achilles in his tent,
Saint Francis praising God:

Hold fast, hold fast to these,
The sturdy and the few
That are more lovely than your love,
More actual than you.

OSTRICH VASE, PRE-DYNASTIC

The shrewd cro-magnon realist
Could set things down as they exist,
Antler and fetlock, hoof and thigh,
With brisk and photographic eye.

The neolithic, coming after,
Could fashion wheel or straighten rafter,
But had no time for idleness,
Thus knowing more and seeing less.

Egypt for the first time on earth
Beheld the line within the girth,
Filling eternity with these
Geometric ostriches.

ELLESMERE ISLAND

This is Thule, this is land's end.
The polar bears walk ponderously on the frozen straits.
Seals bark on the ice floes.
The black ice blinds us.

We have come to the cave of the winds.
We have felt the pulse of the winds with delicate instruments.
We have laid our ears to the great heart of the winds,
Timing the savage valves.

Spring in this country is a red lip kissing the horizon at noon,
And autumn a red mouth kissing good bye to the polar bears and
        their cubs,
And the baby seals with brown puppydog eyes,
Saying, Good night and good luck, I shall be gone a long time.

THE CATS

I saw a thousand cats marching into the west,
Softly on padded paws, making no sound.
The green eyes, like marsh fires, were fixed
Upon the distance, the smooth backs rippled, the tails
Were proud and erect as banners.

Surely, Lord, I said, in all the world
You have made nothing as beautiful as these cats
Marching into the deep west, where the heroes have gone.

THE INSECT HOSPITAL AT AHMEDABAD

Spider, scorpion, gnat, and flea,
Lo, the truth shall make you free.
Through Lord Mahavira's passion
Lie you here in seemly fashion.

Tucked into your little cots,
Bugs and worms and touch-me-nots,
Splintered leg and shattered wing,
Mangled claw and broken sting,

Sleep you fast and rest you well,
Never shall the gates of hell
Prevail against, nor shall death nod
Upon these littlest ones of God.

We will bring you every care,
Tender diet, dainty fare,
Set before you drink and food
Of our bodies and our blood.

TROPICAL FISH IN THE AQUARIUM

These threads of silver, threads of gold,
Slender jewels, crisp and cold
Flowers of sea moss cut the water,
Bent on progeny and slaughter.

The nippled whale, the chinless shark,
The friendly dolphin, and the dark
Monsters on the ocean's bed,
In stateliest procession led

Through vaulted caverns, over rare
Shelves of buried coral, bear
The same relation to their brothers:
Begetting some and eating others.

Thus, unabashed by tank or bowl,
This almost microscopic shoal
Pursue their slight, enameled way,
No less leviathan than they.

from

LONG ISLAND TRIPTYCH AND

OTHER POEMS (1947)

PORTE-BOUTEILLES

The first year of the war Marcel Duchamp,
In a gesture beautiful and lonely,
Exhibited a rack for drying bottles:
The first ready made.

Art had been heading for annihilation
A hundred years. He was the purest eye
Since the industrial revolution. He only
Was in at the kill.

After that it was easy: Dada, the machine cult,
Objects found, objects found and assisted,
Irrational objects and the thoroughly rational:
Cylinder, cone, sphere.

He himself went on for a while wearily:
Bicycle wheel, snow shovel, typewriter cover,
And at last the immortal urinal, the porcelain Buddha,
Signed: R. Mutt, 1917.

But the game was up: he turned to chess and roulette,
Concentric circles on a gramophone table,
One great and final painting, done on glass,
Shattered when finished.

Meanwhile the surrealists continued the pastime:
Vegetable roots, watch springs, boules de neige.
The object departed from its original purity,
Becoming self-conscious.

Politics looked like an out, but it was a sell out.
Dead religions were dug up, in pretty bad shape.
We went back to Gilgamesh, to Altamira, forgetting
The bottle rack.

Abstraction has been reduced to a single line,
The subconscious plumbed, children and idiots heard from,
And the illiterate. The bottle rack stands like a pharos
Over dark waters.

The classic fact has not been superceded.
Escape is impossible, further evasion useless.
The ultimatum has not been replied to,
The word not spoken.

ANGELOLOGY

They come from Persia. The curled ingenuous hair,
The candid nape, the cool and functional arms,
But these are angels and unviolent:
Vestigial wings and long thin fingers playing
Upon the pipes, upon the portative.
This quattrocento stock in trade is found
All over Europe. The Areopagite,
The anchorite converted by St. Paul
Or whoever he was (Justinian quoted him
As an authority before 540)
Set forth for our enlightenment
The nine celestial orders, and thus founded
The noble science of angelology.

Archangels are larger, they loom past you
As you sit drinking coffee in a booth.
Above the powerful throat the bending head
Looks thoughtful but is perhaps only beautiful.
They never accept minor commissions, tots
Lifted brusquely out of a traffic jam
(Who was the nice person that carried me across the street,
Mommy?) they bar the way with flaming swords,
Wrestle with patriarchs, announce important births,
And minister to men with little dogs.
Such occasions however occur but rarely
And are no more than interludes
In their essential and forever burning.

Principalities are dark. The ridged back
Never bends to an explicit task.
They are unapproachable except to the mind
That has forgotten how to suffer.
Otherwise you go blind. The blonde woman
Of obvious Nordic antecedents leans

Across the table, dipping her cigarette
Into the flame cupped by a black palm. Nobody
Notices. This is what I mean. Angels,
Archangels and principalities inhabit
Three interpenetrating planes. Rabbi Akiba
Measured their distance from the throne of God.
Some of them are a third as large as the earth.

Powers are the point beyond which perfection
Becomes meaningless. There is no room left for emotion.
The boy next door, the girl you went to school with:
One comes back to them again and again. A kind of cowardice
To be sure but necessary in the interests
Of sanity. The nervous system
Can take just so much. The tragic view of life
Requires a degree of health that seldom persists
After forty. Hence resignation: In his will
Is our peace. They vary greatly
In size, Sandalfon
Was taller than the others by the length
That one could cover in five centuries of travel.

Virtues are pragmatic and schismatic but never dogmatic.
St. Gregory put them in the third circle, which goes to show
How much more he knew about music than about angels.
The prism is shattered at this point:
The Seminole diving for alligators in the Everglades,
The Sulu diving for pearls at Zamboanga,
The Dane fishing for fish at Ribe,
The Cabra who ran away to join the circus,
And Herbie brought me a quartz crystal from Chatham
Stained to a frail orange by iron oxide,
And a pure sliver of marble.
I am a citizen of no mean planet.
Exit invidia. Amor manet.

Dominions, virtues and powers share one estate.
They occupy the middle ring
Wherein they sing
Glory to God, early and late,
You have to get up early to beat them to it,
Sometimes they sing a trio or a duet,
And sometimes all together, a capella,
Or with the tromba marina, or with continuo
On the clavicembalo,
On trucks or waiting for trucks in alleys,
Climbing subway stairs or waiting for subways
Or walking down 42nd Street,
A neat package tucked under the arm.

Thrones have been over Brooklyn with chromium wings
Reaching from the Pleiades to Orion's right foot,
On clear nights they rise over Prospect Park,
Over the WPA zoo, on the juke box
Tex Ritter is singing Have I Stayed Away Too Long?
We are now approaching so near to the sweetness of God
That words begin to empty themselves of meaning.
A double cheeseburger and a cup of coffee
Come nearer to it than words can ever come,
Hunched at the circus, drinking beer,
Sending out the engraved invitation to the graduation,
Writing the letter: I got married yesterday.
Facts, singing around the throne of God

Continually do cry.
Grotius said the cherubim look like calves, Bochart
And Spencer said they look like bulls, opinions
Stigmatized by Clayton as groundless and infelicitous.
Josephus, being wiser, said that nobody
Has any idea what they look like. Riding the Lexington local,
Roaming the tender fields of Flatbush,

Crossing to St. George on the Gold Star Mother,
My heart breaks. Brands from the burning,
The incised ibex on the stone lamp,
Pallas Athene lifting the cresset before her,
Lighting the dusty armory. Their nature
Is LIGHT.

The river flows between green hills and orange cliffs,
The seraphim afire flow above the river,
The glory of God flows above the seraphim.
Holy Holy Holy they sing,
St. Louis Blues they sing, Blues in the Night they sing.
My heart melts, the marrow in my bones melts.
The glory goes over the city, through the Narrows, past Ambrose
        Lightship.
I saw a nun with a face like a monkey
Catch coins in a cup.
I saw the seraphim receding over New Jersey.
I held out my arms to the wind.
The wind filled my arms, it stuffed my mouth,
It brought voices to my ears.

LAMENT FOR PUERTO RICO

Crossing to Condado, over the long bridge,
The weathered walls of San Geronimo
Were at my left across the bay, the edge
Of the surf pounding over the low
Causeway of rocks. The fishers in the dark
Hung lanterns from the bow.
The lizards in the park,
The royal palms along Ponce de Leon,
The showers that were gone
Before you reached the abandoned sentry box, where the shy,
Giggling couple had preceded you,
And the sudden sun:

In Ponce the byzantine bulbs of the firehouse,
The red uniforms of the firemen's band,
The fountains in the Plaza Central, the sows
Giving suck at every hand:
These and the delicately stepping goats
On the main street in bland
Processional, the boats
At Ponce Playa, and beyond the shore
The still island: no more
Shall these things be except in the heart, no more in the eye,
Nor yield their texture to the lover's hand,
Nor the passionate ear.

Fellé Delgado, the beautiful, the proud,
Will walk across the diamond again
Before a yelling crowd.
Out of a brief rain
The unused sentry box will shelter many a covey of loud
Half-naked children, but not to me
Will it give refuge. The sea

Will shout against the sides of San Geronimo,
But in my ear, only as in a shell,
Held and remembered well,
The slack, the rip, the flow.

THE NIGHTINGALES AT CA' GIUPONE

I heard the first nightingale at mid day.
Climbing the hill to the Rocca, I looked down
Upon the tops of trees
That covered the plain between the Alps and the town.
It was early May,
But not too early for these.
One of them sang while I was standing there
Among the pale
Almond flowers, it came up to me through the clear air
And I said, 'Now I have heard a nightingale.'

But later on, when it was full July,
The trees bore nightingales as cheap as leaves.
I would walk out
To the Feltracco farm at Ca' Giupone,
In one of those cool evenings that give the lie
To the all day sirocco and the heaves
Of heat, after a bout
Of Asti Spumante and pasticcio di macaroni,
Feeling fine, and there would be Mamma Feltracco
Who had had twenty-two children, and when I said,
'How many are living, Signora, and how many dead?'
She smiled and shook her head.
'Non mi ricordo. Ho dimenticato.'
Lupo would be snuffling at my leg,
Whining, and Berto would beg,
'Si sporca tutto, Signor Lino, faccia attenzione.'
But I didn't mind.
Everybody was kind
And I was happy, not knowing what the years were bringing,
And the nightingales were singing and singing and singing,

As they are singing still,
Above the kill.

FIVE PLACES

In Venice I was saved. The second birth
Is not an event but a process. The scission in the psyche
Must knit at last or split from end to end.
I thought I was going to split but I knit instead.
No, Mr. Hubbell, you're not going crazy,
If you were you wouldn't ask me that question.
We had breakfast on the balcony overlooking
The Grand Canal, and late in the afternoon
We went to Torcello to see the great golden Madonna
And I got fleas on the ferry. On the further side
Of the Giudecca, beyond the Dogana and the Salute,
The backyards looked like backyards anywhere.
People called to each other, their voices clear on the water.

In San Juan I was purified. There is peril
In saying, This cannot happen to me again.
And so it happens again and you learn humility,
No other way. And after that you say,
I hope this will not happen to me again,
Walking the razor's edge from that time forth.
The lizards were larger than they were in Italy
But just as shy. Jo got drunk and drove
The wrong way down a one-way street. She found me
Taking a leak under a royal palm
And afterwards we drove to Hato Rey.
It was hotter in Ponce. I walked to Ponce Playa
And saw an island, an island beyond an island.

In Halifax I was empty. Everything
Was in a state of equilibrium.
The British flag flapped outside the Lord Nelson.
I ordered coffee and they sent me tea.
I sent it back. They sent me more tea.
The third time it was coffee. The flag

Drooped. There was a carnival
In a wide field, blaring for half a mile,
And for twenty five cents extra they took off their G strings.
In Yarmouth the Negroes had lawns with no grass on them
And I bought Bacon's essays in a little store
That sold playing cards with the King's and Queen's pictures on them.
There is no hay fever in Nova Scotia.

In 'Sconset I was filled. I was riding high that year,
Life having filled my hands with flowers
Perishable as flowers always are,
Not like the jewel that outlives
The generations of man. The dining room
Was full of retired actresses and xenophobia.
Some of the actresses I remembered, some were before my time.
The xenophobia was also familiar: Portuguese, Armenians and Greeks,
Negroes, Jews and shoeclerks. Shoeclerks
Meant anyone who worked for a living,
But on the beach were pebbles and sandpipers, and pigeons
Looking out of place where the surf crashed. Someone's dog
Followed me all day, having no objection to shoeclerks.

In Perth Amboy I was free. To lose everything,
This is that jewel. Crabbing at Bayard's Beach,
A flat bottomed boat painted blue inside,
White outside except the stern painted blue,
A tin can for bailing, a large can for crabs,
A net. Along the boardwalk to the Raritan Copper Works
With nine miraculously tall and slender chimneys
Looking like a Sheeler. On Smith Street the young people
Stood in the sun doing nothing, like flowers
And almost as perishable. Poseidon,
To the innermost recess of your temple
I bring this crab net. Remember me, God of storms.
Remember me, Amphitrite, when the tide goes out.

READING HISTORY

I would begin with the creation of matter
          out of energy, out of mind, out of God, out of what you will.
Gas condensed in a sphere, and that's the sun.
The sun sideswiped by another, and that's the planets.
The earth cools and hardens, and then the algae
from what you will.
                    Blow, brasses.
                              Life appears.
(Gases, liquids, and solids are beautiful and perfect,
but that's not it.)
I would skip from the algae to the man of Aurignac.
(The beasts are beautiful and perfect,
but that's not it.)
The man of Aurignac, the man of Cro-Magnon,
out of him the arts: all of them, not one missing.
I would skip the neolithic
(the invention of the wheel is not what I'm after)
to pause at Egypt before the Pharaohs came,
where the painter of pots painted the abstract line
in what he saw, and not the thing he saw.

The sun is up, on the Ionian coast
and on the islands of Aeolia:
here Sappho sings pure song, and Thales thinks
pure thought.
                    The sun has cleared the trees.
                              Full day.

Then I would turn
to the chapter after the chapter after the next,
where love is considered simple as eating or sleeping,
where every occupation is respected,
and the vomit of race hatred
                    has been scoured from the pavement.

I read this page over and over, I have turned it down
at the corner, if I drop the book on a table
it opens of itself at this page.

THE BLUE SPRUCE

In the still evening after the hurricane
  The blue spruce is down.
Three times it bowed and three times stood erect,
  Then lay across the lawn.
Though other spruces will usurp its place
  This tree has grown
In death no less mysterious than a man,
  Its whereabouts unknown.

SNOW

Twenty-one years have passed since in another city,
When the first snow was falling as it is falling now,
I walked the evening streets. What was I feeling then?
It is hard to remember in such a different snow.

Twenty-one years and now I am forty-two
And that's just half my life. What has made you stay
When those that I loved later and longer and with greater pain
Are all rejected and put away?

It can't be just that I never had you. Others that I never had
God knows I got over wanting a long while back.
It can't be beauty, though you had that too.
What tangle were you the solution of? what lack?

It must have been the precise hour, the precise minute
Of some infinitely intricate adjustment of the heart,
As a delicate bud that is dipped into liquid gold
Will never open, will never fall apart.

MI FEI

Mi Fei bowed courteously
To the rock in his garden.
He was no ordinary philosopher,
And understood these things.

The cricket whose song
Enchanted his evenings,
The willow which sang
All night when the wind blew,

These he saluted each morning,
But no less the living rock
Which spoke only the one word
Of its identity.

LONG ISLAND TRIPTYCH

one

GREENPOINT

I

The Glory of God shines over Greenpoint.
The oxen of the sun
Tread out the darkness along Newel Street.
The first stenographer announces dawn.
The delicatessens open. It is day.

II

Between Newtown Creek, Bushwick Creek, and East River,
Lies the green peninsula, the green point of land,
Covered with sea green grasses. The Canarsie Indians
Camped here for ages and in 1638
Sold it to the Dutch West India Company from whom
On April 3, 1645,
Dirck the Norman received the patent, whose sons
Sold it to Pieter Praa in 1684
And from that time until the public highway
Was put through in 1838, only
The families of Pieter Praa's daughters: Meserole,
Bennett, Provoost, Calyer, held the land
Where, in the fullness of time, Mae West was born.

The Russians, the Slovaks, the Hungarians
          and the Poles came.
It became part of the town of Bushwick.
The Italians, the Germans, the Irish and the Jews came.
Bushwick became part of the city of Brooklyn.
The refineries, the foundries, the warehouses and
          the gas house came.
Brooklyn became part of the great city,
The wonder of the world. At noon the sun is hot
On Winthrop Park, the colonnade and the angel.
In the side yard of St. Stanislaus the Polish boys
Are playing handball. Along Engert Avenue
From McCarren Park to Fidelity Memorial Park
The Glory of God moves like a procession
With gold fringe, black plumes, and muffled hooves.

III

The heart,
Said Rena,
Must learn to compose, like Palestrina,
Contrapuntally, for many voices,
Each one a separate part.
While one rejoices
Another sweats in anguish.

My dear,
Said Rena,
I suffer for you but I don't worry about you
Because I hear
The contrapuntal texture of your living.
Whatever mess you are in, that goes on without you,
Getting clearer and cleaner.

Essence,
Said Rena,
Is what matters. The rest
Is always either too little or too much.
Sight without touch,
Image without presence
Are good, music without image would be best.

I said
To Rena:
Who am I not to suffer?
I don't wish I were dead
And I don't need a buffer
Between me and hell.
I'm doing all right. I'm getting along quite well.

IV

The human heart is a great institution, I always say.
The prognostic attitude must be abandoned:
This cannot happen to me again cannot be said
Of love, nervous breakdowns, or artistic creation.
The heart of another is a dark forest, said Turgenev.
Who knows the human soul? said Emma Goldman.
You never know which moment will be your next, said the
                    woman in Dorothy Richardson.
The emotional as distinguished from the intellectual nature,
Says Webster's Collegiate Dictionary, Fifth Edition.
Behold thou art fair, my love, behold thou art fair.

The discursive faculty is a fool and a maker of fools:
Shakespeare is a barbarian, Whitman a slob,
Jean-Christophe sentimental slush, etc.
It loves nothing, it understands nothing,
                    it knows nothing.
It is in hell because it does not know it is in hell.
Hell is the absence of suffering.
Incapacity for suffering is damnation.
Indifference to suffering is death.
Give me an ounce of civet, good apothecary,
To sweeten my imagination.

The poet and the mystic are forever apart, but they are
                    friends and not enemies.
The poet aspires toward silence, the mystic achieves it.
The mystic has the firmer will, but the poet
Has the robuster appetite, he wants
To eat his cake and have it too. Hence confusion:
Duchamp turns to chess, Vaché to suicide,
Paul Valéry and Anna Hempstead Branch
To mathematics, Rimbaud to trade,
But none of them turned to silence.
Vivekananda cried out in terror, 'Where is my body?'

V

We see the Germans first in the austere
And lovely prose of Caesar's Gallic War,
On the first page. The Belgae, so he says,
Are bravest of the Gauls because they're near
The Germans who are bellicose, wherefore
The Belgae keep in trim. He says they have
No sacrifices and no priest who prays
To unknown gods, they worship sun and fire
And moon; in other words, what they can see,
The objects of their sight and their desire,
With no Druidic nonsense. Nothing save
Hunting and war concerns them. They are free.

In Tacitus we find them no less free
From Roman government and the austere
Stoic morality, but in him we see
More of their culture. They had all poetry save
The writing down of it (and they were near
The time of runes). This barbarous poetry prays,
Foretells the future and incites to war,
Extolls the magical excellence of fire,
Bays at the moon, howls at the stars, and says
Unspeakable things about the hot desire
Of earth at sowing time. All this we have
Only on hearsay, with its why and wherefore.

But these are modern things. To know wherefore
Man became upright, capable and free,
Behold the earliest German that we have:
Pliopithecus, who came so near
To being a full-fledged gibbon, never prays
To anything at all, is never austere

In act or concept, never wages war
Except to eat or breed. Anthropology says
He lived in the Lower Pliocene. Desire
Lay lightly on his shoulders. He could see
And think no further than he saw, could save
Himself from animals, but had no fire.

The next German may have discovered fire
(Homo Heidelbergensis); how and wherefore
We are ignorant. It is the tongue that prays
And that is lost forever, but we have
The jawbone and the teeth which are very near
To human. It is not likely he was free
From utilitarianism, the desire
For shapeliness in flints, for cooking and war,
Was probably far from him, yet he says
In this hand-ax from Saint-Acheul, that save
The proper human, nothing as austere
Had been designed, and it is here to see.

Next, the Ehringsdorf-Taubach man we see,
Proto-Neandertal, must have had fire,
Must have had manual skill, and seems to have
Aesthetic sense. He seems to have desire
For beautiful objects, witness these austere
And beautiful topaz tools, unfit for war
But exquisite to see. No doubt he prays
To the spirit of his prey, and conjures near
The animal ghosts. The primitive shaman says
The cave-bear and the saber-tooth are free
Without his charm and fetishes, wherefore
The first priest signs the first contract to save.

The true Neandertal was human, save
For the higher arts; in his artifacts we see
A sense of harmony, the flint tools have
Proportion that could only come from desire
To make things comely. Abstract art is near
When the body is painted with manganese. For war
He fashioned axes. When the shaman prays,
He bears the cave-bear's jaw in his austere
And hairy hand. His imagination is free
From the grossest kind of fear. Familiar fire
Burns on his hearth perpetually, wherefore
He waits the lightning. He speaks
                and knows what he says.

Ireland appears in the Mesolithic, says
Science, but there is little enough left, save
Some flints from Larne. The Mesolithic prays
No longer to the beast. The cult of fire
Flourishes and the sun is worshipped. Free
From the nomad's life, man now evolved the austere
Art of the potter, textiles for peace and war,
And microliths, to satisfy the desire
For beauty and utility, wherefore
The Maglemosean pointed bone shafts have
Them fitted in. Just at this time we see
The old age fading and the new age near.

As the end of the Neolithic age drew near
Came megaliths: dolmens, menhirs (which says
'Stone-on-end' in Celtic) and we see
Cromlechs and artificial caves which have
Blankets of earth covered with stones, wherefore
Great tumuli were heaped, for man's desire

To preserve the body was no less austere
Than it became in Egypt. Here he prays
To hafted ax and serpent, still not free
From chthonian terror, but the sun can save
The heart from darkness, and the friendly fire
Disperse the night and the nightmare of war.

Between the stone age and the bronze the war
Of metals passed through copper and gold, drew near
To iron and steel. Copper came first, wherefore
We speak of Chalcolithic, then the austere
And loveliest of metals, gold. Who says
Gold says Ireland. It covered it like a fire.
The Irish fibula spread to Troy that prays
To pre-Homeric gods, became the desire
Of all Europe. In the Iliad we see
The golden socket of Hector's lance. All, save
A little, came from Wicklow, duty-free,
And it was beautiful, and hard to have.

The first American Indian that we have
Is Folsom man. We see him first at war
With giant bison, peccary we see,
Sloth, camel, horse and antelope. Wissler says
He is Mesolithic, had the use of fire,
Was nomad, without pottery, with austere
Absence of decoration. Certainly prays
To something, limited use of bone, wherefore
He lagged behind Crô-Magnon. The desire
For durable baskets must have brought him near
To pottery but he never reached it, save
Possibly here and there: surmise is free.

The Poosepatuck Indians roam free
At Mastic where the salt winds blow. They have
Radios and have long since conquered fire,
Gas and electricity. They are near
Neighborhood movies, but the guide book says
Their blood is mixed with African, wherefore
The Shinnecocks, further out on the island, see
No reason to cultivate them, they desire
To remain unmixed, continuing the war
On racial tolerance. When will the austere
Voice of reason reach this island and save
The wretch who hates, the hypocrite who prays?

In Greenpoint only the broken hearted prays,
Prowling the streets at midnight, but the free
Frequent pool parlors, frequently they have
Tail in the park. The social worker says
They are a problem, being too dull to see
That only in this way they are able to save
Themselves from going completely nuts, wherefore
They are wise to warm themselves before the fire
Built in an ashcan, and to huddle near
Each other in the apathetic war
With death. Only when they are filled with desire
Are they beautiful, and in some strange way austere.

Who once was free and now is filled with desire,
Who burns in fire and can no longer see
To whom he prays, to whom he would draw near,
Cries out and says, it is better to have what I have,
To be thus at war with death, than to be the austere
Who know how to save themselves, who know wherefore.

VI

As I turned into Newel Street
The gas house smelled as plain
As when you were a child, and there
Was the old smell again,

And people that I never knew
Came crowding on the wind
Like drunken ghosts, their faces pale
Wavering and thinned,

But there was one who stood apart
And fixed me with a stare,
More beautiful than all the rest
And more than I could bear.

VII

The light that shines at the center of the universe,
The flame that burns at the center of existence,
The fire that glows at the center of my being,

The tranquility of Brancusi's bird,
Of Mondrian's great black and white diamond,
Of Debussy's clouds,

This is my home, this is where I live,
I have stayed away too long,
I must try to go back.

The wafers of triple bromide in the medicine cabinet,
The luminol, the phenobarbitol,
The codeine hangover,

The horrible dream in which you think you wake up
                and find it is still true.
The fear of going to bed, the cup of hot milk,
The long walks at night,

The coffee in counter joints on Driggs Avenue
At four in the morning, the lousy sandwiches,
The dirty cup,

The hysteria, the clowning, the embarrassment,
                the repeated pattern,
The renewed attempt, the discouragement, the shame,
The continued failure,

The humiliation of the mind, of the heart,
                of the flesh, of the intention,
The taste of self hatred sour in the throat
Like vomit,

The literary men who hate Shakespeare, the scholars
                who hate life,
The artists who hate each other,
                the bitching of one 's friends,
The political row,

The religious crap, the mystic cult, the phony messiah,
The dull lecture, the frustrated and jealous women,
The fake experience,

The loud bullshitting in the pool rooms
                and the bowling alleys,
The unfunny joke, the two packs of butts a day,
The bum liquor,

It is all good, I would not unlive a moment of it,
I do not disown a moment of it,
I thank God for it,

But it has taken me far from the center of my being
Where there is sound within silence and silence
                within sound
And light within darkness.

I have been gone long enough. I have not forgotten
The way nor the direction. I shall go back
This time to stay,

And in that place where the air is unstirred
                and untroubled
The wolves of confusion, disorder and excess
Will fall dead at your feet.

VIII

Anaptomorphus Homunculus
The tiny primate

Lived in North America
During the Eocene

Resembling the lemurs
Of Malaya

And the tarsioids
Of Madagascar

With short muzzle
And large brain

Before the ice sheet
Passed over Long Island

Before Pliopithecus
Chattered across Germany

Before Propliopithecus
And Parapithecus

Lived in the Fayum:
En ce temps-là le désert était peuplé d'anachorètes.

IX

Why are these people indifferent?

They are indifferent because they are ignorant.

But why are they ignorant? In every city,
Town and village there is a public library,
And though they are tired when night comes they are
                    not too tired
For radios and movies, for bridge and comic strips.
Why then do they remain ignorant?

They are ignorant because they lack curiosity.

Is not a lack of curiosity indifference?
Is this a vicious circle?

No.
Real indifference is knowing and not caring.
Lack of curiosity is not caring to know.
They do not care to know.

                              Emily Dickinson said,
My mother does not care for thought.

              Precisely.
But why?

Because they lack imagination.
From lack of imagination comes lack of curiosity.
From lack of curiosity comes ignorance.
From ignorance comes indifference, or what seems
Indifference. Being without imagination,
No bomb is real except the one that hits them.

What can be done about lack of imagination?

That is the artist's job.

The artist has no job except to be an artist.
It is the educator's job to use wisely
What the artist has done.

It is the parent's duty to choose for teachers
Men and women with imagination.

But the parents have been corrupted by their parents
And do not care. Children are taught in school
To respect science but not art.
The grocery clerk laughs at the artist
Which puts the artist at a disadvantage:
An artist cannot laugh at a grocer's clerk.
Meanwhile science kills its tens of millions
Which art could have saved,
                    whether the artist wished to or not.

But under feudalism art was respected,
And without science men managed to kill each other.

To respect art is a great deal but it is not enough.
To understand art is to awaken the imagination
From which comes all the rest.

Can you make everyone understand art?

Why not? We have come a long way
From Anaptomorphus Homunculus.
When did the process end:
                    last night at midnight?

Who can set bounds for man's growth?
You must have the patience of God
In whose sight a thousand years are but as yesterday.
God can afford to be patient, I cannot.

I am not patient. I am a realist.
I do not expect a child three months old
To understand Beethoven's last quartets.

Then you have faith?

                              Only in what I see.

X

In early middle age
There comes a quiet time
When you think the fight is won.

It has not even begun.

The fire roars in the wood,
The tide rises higher
Than you thought it ever could.

two

RIDGEWOOD

I

All the nine kinds of angels sing
Over Ridgewood in the spring,
The stoops are scrubbed, the steps are washed,
The pavements clean, the gutters flushed,
The boys and girls are dressed to kill,
The reservoir is on top of the hill,
The jive comes hot, the jive comes sweet
On Linden Street, on Linden Street,
And beauty sneaks up without warning
In Ridgewood on an April morning.

The Mespatches Indians lived where now in Ridgewood
German burgers drink beer, attend the Turnverein,
The Sangerbund, the movies, listen to the radio,
The English settled the Ridge in the seventeen hundreds,
Looking down across Maspeth: English, Dutch, Quakers,
Ridgewood does not appear on Conner's map,
But in Beers' atlas it is a part of Newtown.
It now lies partly in Brooklyn and partly in Queens.

The houses are all alike but what goes on
Inside the houses is never twice the same,
Life being inexhaustible, or if the same
It is different in every person it goes on in.
Even to the same person love is different
Each time it happens, and the fear of death
Waxes and wanes with other circumstance.
Only the house fronts need numbers to be distinguished.

Crossing St. Nicholas Avenue you are in Queens.
The streets are broad, leaving plenty of space
For the sun to shine. Here and there an ailanthus
Splits its coarse orange bud and puts out green
As delicate as ferns. The romanesque
Church of St. Brigid stands at the borough line,
The German names on the delicatessen windows
Interrupted by pizzerias and olive oil.

The idiot boy and his brother, hardly more than an idiot,
Go hand in hand down the street where a mind
As clear and cold as the ice cave of Amarnath
Writes poems, makes drawings, plays the piano:
The wind bloweth where it listeth. He said,
My uncle remembers when there were cows all over Ridgewood.
When I was little he took me to the Grove to the fights,
I can still remember how the smoke hurt my eyes.

III

Play Czerny to me. It says arithmetic,
Clearness with rapidity,
The passing under of the thumb,
Play it until your thumb is numb,
On you it looks good.

Play me the School of Velocity
With dispatch and ferocity
The way a woodpecker would.
Better play safe and play Czerny,
It says nothing at all.

Stick to Czerny. Above all
Do not play what Liszt made of the scene
Of love and death at the obscene
Height of the romantic movement.
This is all I can take.

I am hanging on the ropes but I know
They won't break
Because I twisted them myself and I know
Just how much they can take,
But it's better not to take any chances.

So play Czerny until your fingers drop off,
I'm a tough old bastard but there are limits,
And never mind your engulphed cathedrals,
Your gardens in the rain,
Or even the white peacock: I know when I've had enough.

Go up the scale and down the scale,
Let your thumb pass under and your fingers pass over,
And I hope to God I'm far away
When you learn to play
Beethoven.

IV

The true mystic has no truck with art,
The phenomenal universe being annihilated.
These atheists of art: Vaché, Duchamp,
Are like the American Association for the Advancement of Atheism
Which meets on Sunday afternoon to denounce religion.
They are afire with religion. If they were not
They would be at a ball game or a movie, not there.
But mysticism annihilates religion itself,
Which is why St. Theresa got in trouble.
The mystics of art: Mondrian, Malevich,
Go only half way, end in a compromise.

The artist may be religious, but not a mystic:
Roualt is a great religious painter, Rembrandt a greater,
But mysticism is found elsewhere:
In the quiet of Quakers, the silence of Zen Buddhists,
The Nirvikalpa Samadhi of the Advaitins,
The Tao which if it is the true Tao is not the Tao,
Essenes, Quietists and Sufis. I asked a Japanese
Whose father was a Shinto priest if the Shintoists
Meditated. Yes, he said, they meditate all right.
Well, I said, what do they meditate on?
They just sit quietly, he said.

The Digambara Jains go naked and cremate themselves
Eventually, they wear cloths over their mouths
To avoid the slaughter of insects, at Ahmedabad
They have a hospital for wounded bugs.
Joseph Cornell put watch springs in a pill box
And dedicated it to Marcel Duchamp.
Art, religion and mysticism are confused
In this passion for purification and annihilation
That drove Rimbaud to Africa and Walter Conrad Arensberg
To Hollywood, 'As far away from New York
As we could get without crossing the ocean.'

V

A million centuries before the first
Primate was born, a terrible race of creatures
Ran, jumped and hopped, in hunger and in thirst,
Across Long Island. Horrible to see,
Worse to encounter, they were the best of nature's
Efforts so far, which was enough to be.

A dinosaur's a noble thing to be
Compared with a trilobite. It was not the first
Nor was its fate to be the last of nature's
Experiments with life, but never were creatures
So large again. It is not hard to see
Why she abandoned them to hunger and thirst.

Yet out of predatory and sexual thirst
They produced an object which to this day can be
Admired for its beauty. It is possible to see
A spiral clutch of eggs, laid by the first
Armoured dinosaur, one of the creatures
Called Protoceratops. The art is nature's.

Elongated and ellipsoidal, their nature's
More like a bird's than a reptile's. All the thirst
For self perpetuation of these creatures
Now turned to solid sandstone, they can be
Admired but not hatched. They are not the first
Vertebrate eggs that have lived for us to see.

From the Redbeds of western Texas we can see
An egg that is twice as old: in the course of nature's
Experiments in the Permian age the first
Reptiles laid eggs like this, the instinctive thirst
For continuance functioning as it was to be
World without end, in these archaic creatures.

In the Tertiary, among new fangled creatures
With wings, which had discarded teeth, we see
The Aepyornis' egg, which lived to be
Preserved in Elie Faure. This feat of nature's,
Like a Brancusi, satisfies the thirst
For beauty, while putting procreation first.

In the red sandstone of Massachusetts the first
Carniverous dinosaurs, saber-toothed creatures,
Have left their footprints. Driven on by thirst,
They left attenuate marks for us to see
Like dried and curling leaves, preserved by nature's
Trick of petrefaction, which let them be.

Now in park and museum they can be
Examined at our leisure. We are the first
Of sentient beings to examine nature's
Enormous panorama and her creatures
With curiosity and intent to see
What appetite compelled them, and what thirst.

We are no different in our hunger and thirst
Except for our ability to be
At the same time objective and to see
What makes us suffer, having suffered first.
We are most helpless and most glorious creatures,
Being at once God's progeny and nature's.

After the dinosaurs had passed in nature's
Recondite procession, led by thirst
No less acute there came placental creatures,
Ungulate and herbivorous, to be
Ancestors of the elephant, the first
Mammoth and mastodon and bison we see.

Thus from original reptile to man we see
Inexorable intention, which is nature's.
The higher from the lower, the last from the first
Forever and forever, this subtle thirst
Produces from what is what is to be
In a succession of improving creatures.

Now on the streets of Ridgewood other creatures,
Placental and omnivorous, we see,
Primates with tear ducts, and content to be,
For the most part, no other thing than nature's
Archaic and uncomplicated thirst
Intended them to compass from the first.

Who is not the first nor yet the last of creatures
Who endures thirst and bitterness, can see
That he is nature's, and is content to be.

three

GLENDALE

I

Sun and rain fall gently over Glendale,
The light is sweet
On 67th Street.

New moon and Venus glowing over Glendale,
And after dark
Desire prowls the park.

II

Glendale is happy because it has no history.
It lies between the cemetery and the railroad tracks
And nobody has ever written a book about it.
It first appears in the eighteen seventies
As part of Newtown.

The wind roars in the underpass entering Glendale,
All at once the houses are low and even.
The concrete cylinders of the coal company
Like the columns of Karnak stand above the tracks,
Egyptian and important.

Beyond the coal company the steel frame
Of the power station, with the sky showing through,
Delicately balanced, candid and reticent,
Resembles the Palace at 4 A.M.
By Giacometti.

In J. Wesley Drumm Park a glacial boulder,
Split in half, a bronze plaque fastened
To its wounded side, celebrates
A pioneer educator, for once apparently not
A contradiction in terms.

The necropolis stretches for miles with small pretentious
Marble huts for the useless dead, just as useless
When they were alive. The living live in rows
Of unpretentious and identical houses, who will be
Isolated in death.

The monument makers' yards are filled with slices
Of marble waiting for names to be cut on them,
Names of men and women and children
Now walking around Glendale, not suspecting
The association.

In the windows are pots of cacti and succulents,
With little imitation Japanese gardens,
Regardless of current hates, so strong the inertia
Of middle class taste, indifferently
Stuck into the dirt.

V

In the Devonian, Long Island was under water.
Fish were its most advanced inhabitants,
Appearing first, intent on love and slaughter,
During this age. Under the narrow sea
Crawled the crustacean, limited of sense,
And molluscs, contented not to crawl but be.

Majestically, where Glendale was to be,
The paddled Antiarchi cleft the water.
The jawless Placodermi, with less sense,
Were put upon by the inhabitants
Of this prolific and ferocious sea,
Having barely time to breed before their slaughter.

The acanthodians, as adept at slaughter
As sharks are now, had little else to be
Except eating or eaten, while the sea,
Deepened and widened, and beneath the water
Limestone was laid down. The inhabitants
Continued to grow in action and in sense.

In action more resourceful and in sense
More intricate, in breeding and in slaughter
Always more complex, the inhabitants
Of these fierce channels gradually came to be
Ready for the day when they would leave the water.
Some left it, others lingered in the sea.

Some of them to this day are in the sea,
While others, more evolved in mind and sense,
Inhabit Glendale. These who left the water
Have made an art of love, a science of slaughter,
And have developed things that would not be
Intelligible to the sea's inhabitants.

I that am one of the inhabitants
Of land should never have strayed so far from sea.
I would be better off if I could be
As sharp of instinct and as dull of sense,
As limited to progeny and slaughter
As these quick shadows in Long Island water.

Long Island water and its inhabitants,
Their love and slaughter in the shadowy sea,
The untroubled sense, are as they ought to be.

VII

There are three stages of consciousness.
The first is waking, the ambiance of love,
The second dream, the subterranean source.
The life of animals is a perpetual dream.
The third is dreamless sleep, which we share
With minerals and the dead.
This is the impartial and promiscuous soil
In which our individual thoughts and dreams
Are rooted. Mystics call it Anima Mundi.
No Cretan snake god ever dug so deep.
Minerals live this life, which makes them beautiful
Whether in mountains or on museum shelves.
They are the quiet kingdom, living nearest
To the great soul of the world.

It is impossible to imagine
The unflawed purity of such an existence.
Love and its suffering, born of separation,
Cannot exist where there is no separation.
Religion ceases to have significance
Where perfect union has been achieved.
As for the negation of the phenomenal
Which haunts the modern artist, here it is.
Mysticism's dream is realized
Where the rain falls on granite, and neither rain
Nor granite knows that the rain falls on granite,
Nor granite that it is granite, nor rain rain,
Because such knowledge implies separateness.
This is the kingdom of the dead as well.
Those are pearls that were his eyes.

The marble and the man beneath the marble
Share one purity. Is it possible
To achieve this perfection without dying
Or being a mineral? Buddha says it is.

Confucius says, At fifteen I wanted to learn.
At thirty I stood on my own feet.
At forty my doubts were destroyed.
At fifty I knew the will of God.
At sixty my ears accepted tranquilly
Whatever they heard.
At seventy I could do as I pleased without sinning.

VIII

In the Cambrian
Before the fish came

Radiolarian
Arrow worm

Trilobite
Limpet

Jelly fish
And sponge

Inhabited
Greenpoint

Ridgewood
And Glendale

X

The voice of the ocean will be the same,
                    year in and year out
The stars will not alter their appearance
                    in the night sky.
The heart is stronger than anything that
                    can happen to it.

from

SEVENTY POEMS

(PART ONE)

(1965)

BUKOBA

When storms rage on Victoria Nyanza
Hammering against the piers of Bukoba
The rector of the Anglican church
Is disturbed in his devotions, but the crocodiles
Are quite unmoved, in fact they rather
Enjoy it. The Arabs accept it
As an inscrutable gesture on the part of
Allah, the Compassionate, the Merciful.

The herons, fearful for their delicate
Feathers, huddle among the reeds.
The natives simply lie down and go to sleep.
The tsetse flies simply lie down and go to sleep
In the natives. Thus do all creatures,
After their kind, respond
To the inscrutable gesture of
Allah, the Compassionate, the Merciful.

THE FIRST ARCHITECT

The valves of the diatom are sculptured,
But you cannot see them. You cannot even
See the diatom, and yet
Its convex walls of silica, two shells
Which fit each other neatly as a pill box
Fits the pill box cover, are wrought
With no less concentration
Than the Apollonian pediment at Olympia,
And may be bought for half a buck
To look at under a microscope.
O wonder, half a buck for something you can't see
Until you take it home and put it on a slide:
An invisible plant building its invisible house.

The curtains have parted, this is a far cry
From colloids and carbon compounds.
The individual has appeared.
You can say, 'It begins here.
It ends there.' Something has happened all right,
A conscious shaping, and (this is the tip off)
No two alike. Spheres, crescents and queer shreds,
Like something by Rudolph Bauer. We are still,
After a billion years of biological evolution,
Doing the same thing. We are consciously
Making forms. Making form.
An invisible plant making its invisible house,
A man painting (just as invisible doubtless
To a grosser eye: Moholy-Nagy
Placed on a slide for half a buck
Would be seen doing the same thing:
Consciously making forms. Making
Form.) They live in fresh water
Or salt water with equal complacence.
Their walls are of opal.

One hundred and twenty million of them
Weigh an ounce. They are without number.
Their opaline and sculptured walls,
An invisible plant making its invisible house,
Are where you have to begin if you want to understand
Art. Consciously making forms. Making form.

ORDOVICIAN FOSSIL ALGAE

This is the oldest book
That I can read with pleasure.
The Cambrian trilobite
Is an unpleasant sight.
As for Pre-Cambrian algae I look and look
And cannot see them, though I'm told they're there.

But these
Exquisite fern-like forms
Printed upon the rock,
These fragile plants that have survived the storms
Of some odd billion years
Move me almost to tears.

So I come here often
To see these delicate stems
Breathed on the rock like frost crystals on a window,
But permanently,
But forever.
This rock is my favorite book, my favorite picture,
My dependable scripture,
My sense of wholeness, a billion years at my elbow.

COUTCHICHING SCHIST

This is the oldest rock
in North America
before bacteria
at midnight on the clock
of geologic time
before the alga
caught in magma
secreted lime
these contorted
sediments were made,
these distorted
layers were laid
at Mile 6
on the Canadian Northern.
Earth's burden
of life was new
that now sticks
in her maw.

FORAMINIFER

The foraminifer is ameboid
But like the snail
Secretes a hard calcareous shell
And lives therein,
Visible to the unassisted eye,
Being no smaller than the head of a pin.

It dies in rain upon the ocean floor
One third of which is paved
With foraminifer's abandoned house.
The trilobite, which is a sort of louse,
Has been extinct these many million years
But foraminifer,

Its Cambrian contemporary,
This exquisite, just visible architect,
Still falls, like snow within a boule de neige,
Upon the stormless bottom of the sea,
Leaving in layer on layer
Its chalky heritage.

THE COURTSHIP OF THE ANNELIDA

The bristle-worms, marine and segmented,
Take places for the dance.
This is the primal mime, preceding far
Rococo and romance.

The males wriggle in rows, the females watch,
Nubile and excited.
Compared with this the partridge's pavane,
The grouse's gavotte are modern and sophisticated.

From this original came Cro-Magnon ritual
Accompanied upon the cave-bear's jaw,
The passion of Osiris and Dionysus,
Shakespeare, and Shaw.

MALEVICH

You put a pencilled square on a piece of paper,
And then a circle, off center, then two squares
Perfectly balanced, and the public cried out in terror:
We are lost.
At last, having purified the intellect beyond example,
You painted a white square, on a diagonal axis,
In cool white, on a background of warm white,
Calling it White on White.
Those were the morning days, after the great revolution,
When the poet stood on the platform without speaking,
And came down, saying: That was my poem,
Which is silence.
But the going was rough, and Lenin said:
This is a disorder of Leftism, let us have no more nonsense.
Movies are what we need, posters and book jackets,
And sets for the theatre.
Something must have gone wrong: it is the intellectuals
Who reject you now, it is the new smartness to laugh
At your sort of thing. Who better than a simple person
Could understand a square?
Martyr who died in bed, entirely artist,
The circle and the square are impregnable.
They will survive a great deal of talking,
And a good many laughs.

MONDRIAN

Three flower pieces done in nineteen six
Show the object receding already.
Cubism freed the line
But he went on looking for the single, incredible thing,

Granted to only a few out of a generation:
The key to the private door, the word list
Of a language not worn out
By a million egotistical mouths, by a tribe of talkers.

It happened, to him uniquely among so many,
At the moment in which hope was abandoned,
The miracle awaited with fear,
Without possible explanation it happened.

Mathematician and saint, these pure canvases
Answer the question that a desperate generation
Had put to itself. It is no longer necessary
For a serious man to renounce art.

JACQUES VACHÉ

With murder and suicide you ended what Rousseau began.
The break with the classical tradition was complete.
It was not enough to go trading in Abyssinia:
The romantic movement had been a reaffirmation
Of life against art, in the narrow sense, but the revolution
Once started went headlong, it was not enough
To say: l'art est une sottise, the sickness spread
From member to member, until life itself became
Suspect, rejected, the ultimate sottise.
By what curious process did revolt against the neo-classic
Begin with Rousseau and with you, Jacques Vaché?

When you killed your friend with much applauded wit,
And yourself with an admired gesture, a sly overdose,
You negated everything once and for all; your disciples,
The dadaists, not wishing to die, were shown up as pikers:
Pierre de Massot said that he went on living
For love of death, which was rhetoric. He went on living,
Having his picture taken with hat on one side,
A cigarette in the corner of his mouth, tough as all hell,
But living and writing and becoming a communist,
Just as if everything were not a sottise, just as if
You had never negated everything, Jacques Vaché.

But perhaps you were right after all, say you ended
Art based on the conscious and the subconscious mind,
Seeing that there was nothing more to be done on those levels.
Below the subliminal mind of the individual,
The world of dream and hypnogogic illusion,
Lies the clear anima mundi without boundaries.
It has no language, none that we can spell,
But nothing less will content us in the end.
Are you laughing, Jacques Vaché, you that now share
The great unconsciousness of the minerals
And the omniscience of the universe?

SAPPHICS ON AN ASHTRAY IN THE SHAPE OF A PIANO

Pigmy toy made to look like piano
You are absurd with your keys all in one piece,
Anachronistic in a time given to
    Functionalism

An ashtray should look like an ashtray, never
By any circumstance like a piano.
In an age of taste you would be found in a
    Chamber of horrors

Along with the famous porcelain Venus,
The butt of so many jokes, now a cliché,
But still harboring the stopped and inutile
    Clock in her belly.

HALF CENTURY

From nineteen ten to nineteen twenty
There was art and art aplenty.
From nineteen twenty to nineteen thirty
Experiment was confined
To the unconscious mind.
From nineteen thirty to nineteen forty
Economics ruled the roost,
Superseding Freud and Proust.
Since then there's been a general rout,
Courage has given out
And poets home, like well trained pigeons,
To various obsolete religions.

SECRET WEAPON

I looked up to the sky and saw it there,
Not really saw, for it was made of glass
Or some plastic like glass
And only a faint suggestion of the perimeter
Was visible where the sun's rays hit the rim.

But there it was filling half the sky,
Invisible except where the reflected light
Glanced off the edge:
The inevitable, the diabolical
End of invention, the weapon perfected in darkness.

It has come, I said, and I tried to take courage
By remembering the countless dead that have died in the past,
But that did no good, I was afraid,
I was filled with anger and despair
As I waited, helpless, looking up at the sky.

ANT HILL

When little ranges of ant hills
Appeared along the cracks of the sidewalks
The maid would come out with a kettle
And pour boiling water on them.

The ants all perished,
Writhing briefly in the scalding torrent,
Then dissolving slowly as it settled.
They never knew what hit them.

AFTER

The grass will not perish, and in far, forgotten places
Trees will grow strong in the sun, will sing in the rain.
On unfrequented lakes the lily pads
Will tug at the tough anchor.

The striped onyx and the watery amethyst
Will burn unquenched within the quiet hill.
Ridges of granite and ledges of marble will bear
The weight of wind and wave.

The fine sand and the coarse along the shore
Will rustle at the tide line, where the sandpipers
Among the purple drifted eelgrass run
With mincing human steps.

GEMINI

Being born under the difficult sign
Of Gemini that brings
Division to the soul, I hesitate
Between two things
Not knowing which is mine.

In me the weight
Of elements is at such equipoise
Neither exceeds the other by a dram,
And so I see two faces in the glass
Uncertain which I am.

DREAMS

Bodies as brief as waves, uncertain identities,
Men and women that inhabit my changing dreams,
What mysterious existence is yours that act
Without reason, speak strange words, and love,
Out of the dark wells of my unrecognized
Fears and desires?

Are you, in the short interval of your activity,
Aware of a continuity outside of my dream?
Are you indeed projections of my importance,
Or am I rather a collection, held loosely together,
Of shaken leaves, of easily broken stems,
And you the enormous root?

UNDERSEA

Under the wave and a long way under
Far below the ebb and the flow,
Beneath the sound of the surface thunder,
Beyond the reach of the undertow,
Grow the anemones, lies the lonely,
Long abandoned, forgotten freight,
And there abide such creatures only
As can endure the weight.

ENERGY

Of the unnumbered forms
That energy assumes,
Three have I always loved:
Cats, cacti, and stones.

A cat can live alone
Or gracious at the hearth,
Gregarious at will,
Unmastered to the death.

The cactus grows in soil
Of little nourishment.
It thrives on what would mean
Death to another plant.

As for a stone, smoothed
By the sea, and wind-scoured,
Who would not wish to be
So tempered and so hard?

TREE

Leaving Brattleboro, I looked across at the hills
On the New Hampshire side.
At the top of one of them, against the sky,
A tree stood.

There were no other trees near it, though the woods grew thick
All the way up the climb.
It was the first living thing I had opened my heart to
In a long time.

I said, I shall remember this tree as long as I live,
No matter what else I see.
I watched it through the train window until we moved away,
But it was unconscious of me.

CANADIAN SPRUCE

The Canadian Spruce is straight and tall,
Taller than the house.
They are cutting it down.
In the autumn weather
They are cutting it down
Because its needles fall into the gutters of the roof
And interfere with the plumbing.

ALLIGATOR SONG

Its voice is
gentle, and it grieves
Like pigeons in the caves.
How sweet a note
Within the valved, amphibious throat.

There is no hatred in the eyes
And no surprise.
Life is diffused throughout the alligator
By its creator,

Not focused in the brain.
Comfort it vaguely feels, and vaguely pain,
And, in the hour of love,
Coos like a dove.

PYTHON

I stroked a python once. The keeper said:
Folks think they're cold and slimy, but they aren't at all.
I felt, and under my astonished fingers
Flowed my own life, familiar and comfortable.

PIGEON

I looked in the ashcan to see if there was room
To empty my baskets, and there on the bottom
Lying on its side was a pigeon,
Its dead eye open and looking straight up,
Obviously seeing nothing.

I lifted a basket, but before burying
The bird in hugger-mugger
I looked it in the eye. The eyes met,
Living and dead, but nothing passed between them.
The connection had been cut.

WHALE

You cannot keep
a pet whale

unless you have
an ocean.

NIGHT PIECE

Night clears.
The islands of the sky
Come out, and the nearer stars.
The moon is high,
Touching each tree
And every hill with light.
We do not ask for day,
But for a clear night.

THEOGONY

In the beginning was Chaos,
says Hesiod in the Theogony,
then rose great-bosomed Earth,
and Love.

Now, like a strip of film run backward,
Love goes,
and Earth about to be devoured
by her own vermin,

and in the end
as it was in the beginning,
Chaos,
the first god and the last.

from

ATLANTIC TRIPTYCH (1971)

PART ONE

I

AD MAJOREM DEI GLORIAM
Who spread the sea
On all sides of the land, and at the bottom
Planted gardens of sea-
Cucumbers and lilies, where shrimps
With long legs live at a great depth
Among the glass sponges and the enormous
Monocanthus. Neither tide nor wind
Touches them. Light never changes.
Temperature never varies. Pressure,
Being always equal, is unfelt.
Food floats down like rain
From the upper waters.

Along the coast
Grow the brown algae: rockweed, grapeweed,
Broad-leaved sargassum, and kelp
A hundred feet long.
The frailer red algae
Grow further out, deeper
Than sun reaches. Drifting on the surface
Lies the uncountable unicellular plankton:
Diatoms, changing shape with the seasons,
Dinoflagellates, making
The Red Sea red, and smaller still
The coccolithophoridae that shun
The polar ocean.

Rays and chimaeras range
From Norway to Sumatra. Eels are spawned
Southeast of Bermuda.
When they are eight
They come from Europe and America

Fighting their way downstream, swimming
Tirelessly thousands of miles
To the spawning ground. Pipe fish, needle fish,
Sea horse and stickleback
Nose through the eel grass, or hide
Inside the sea-cucumber.
The flute-mouth
Hunts off shore in the warm equatorial waters.

III

The noble island of Lesbos
Which is smaller than Long Island
Has produced more major poets
Than all of the United States.
Terpander, the great musician,
Arion, a tragic poet
A hundred years before Thespis,
Sappho of course and Alcaeus,
Lesches, the writer of epic,
And other illustrious men,
Pittacus, one of the Seven
Wise Men of Greece, and the severed
Head of Orpheus was carried
By waves to the shores of Lesbos.
Homer himself celebrated
The fair cheeked daughter of Phorbas.

VI

On April 13, 1660,
Major General Harrison
Was hanged, drawn, and quartered.
Mr. Pepys, who was present at the entertainment,
Wrote in his diary,
'He looked as cheerful as any man would look in that condition.'
Pepys was an ordinary person
Which is why so many ordinary people love him.

But Mozart was not ordinary.
On November 30, 1770,
When he was in Milano
Waiting for the first performance of
Mitridate, Rè di Ponto,
He wrote in a letter,
'I saw four rogues hanged today in the Piazza del Duomo.
They hang them here the same way they do at Lyon.'

VII

Alcman came to Sparta from the East,
Bringing Aeolian grace and Ionian wit
To the city of the boy who fed the beast

Under his coat, for in those days it was thought fit
For a great city to have a great poet.
He took the choral ode, divided it,

Strophe, antistrophe, epode, and in order to show it
To best advantage, he himself trained the boys
Who were going to dance it and the girls who were going to play it,

Disguised as doves, and owls with round eyes.
He loved the ceryl, the cock halcyon
Skimming the purple waves, he loved the noise

Of partridges, he loved the summer moon,
Dew on the deergrass, and he loved to eat
A country supper of cheese and honey, none

Of your fancy food for him, he loved the sweet
Wine of Carystus, he loved the parted thighs
Of girls, but most of all he loved the great

Silence that lies on mountains and on seas
When all things turn to sleep, whales in the ocean,
Birds, animals, and the generation of the bees.

Sappho felt the teeth of sexual passion
Worry her flesh as no one ever did.
She knew the intellectual emotion

Of shaping words and abstract sound, she made
The pektis, that was played without a quill,
Popular in the islands (Alcman had played,

First in all Greece, the magadis.) Her will,
Holding its own with desire, as it must
In the hour of longing, imposed the beautiful

Restraint of art upon the cry of lust
That rose to her lips at the sight of a young body
In its short time of perfection. The heart's thirst

Has never spoken before or since with such steady
Dignity, with such controlled force,
Or such miraculous form. She drank the heady

Draught of the world, she tracked it to its source
On sunny hillsides where the breezes flail
The apple branches by the water course,

Or where the golden pulse grows by the shale
That washes in from Asia, or the moon
Rising at midnight makes the stars turn pale.

Alcaeus was a Tory and a fighting man.
Unlike Sappho, he preferred pleasure to ecstasy.
Wine and boys were his dish. He was the bane

Of Pittacus and fought for the nobility
Against the democratic party. He went
Into exile, rather than truckle to the new

Government of Lesbos. Bitter and arrogant
He sent back satires to Mitylene as vicious
As any that Archilochus had penned,

But in the end he came home, the sagacious
Tyrannus having pardoned him. His virile
Poems, magnificent but a bit sententious,

Resemble Horace, only better. Being in peril
At the battle of Sigeum, he threw away
His shield, not caring greatly for the quarrel

With Athens. He lived to fight another day
And joked about it. His verse forms were a bonanza
To the Latin poets. All the ancients say

He was a great musician. The extravaganza
Of his life is given a certain dignity
By what he did for metrics and the stanza.

Anacreon preferred fun to pleasure or ecstasy.
The cult of Eros was growing less devout,
The lion's claw changing to the barb of the bee.

He came to Samos to teach the lyre and the lute
To Polycrates, spending his time in frolics,
Drinking, kissing, playing the half-bore flute,

Throwing the cottabus, writing Aeolian lyrics
In Ionian dialect, songs as crisp as lettuce,
Fresher than any written since, save Herrick's.

Sometimes, when Sicilian wine had made his head as
Light as the Teian air, the thought of death
Would cross his mind. He'd think, 'I'll be as dead as

Sappho one of these days.' It would catch his breath
For a minute, then he'd take another drink,
Kiss Cleobulus again, make an act of faith

In his lucky star, and forget again to think.
Most of the poems that profit from his fame
Aren't his at all, but even so they rank

With the best in the songbooks of Elizabeth's time.
He choked on a grape when he was eighty five,
And Athens raised a statue to his name.

Stesichorus followed Alcman, one of the grave
Dorian line, but Alcman had come from the east
And never became a bee in the Spartan hive,

As he did. Taking the choral ode, he fused
Its lyric grace with epic majesty
Taken from Homer, recast the myths, unfazed

By orthodox religion, adumbrated tragedy,
Wrote love stories in verse, in anticipation
Of the Greek Romance, and made a bestiary

Of fables with political connotation.
He was impersonal without being cold.
Somehow he fell between the stools of narration,

Derived from Homer, Hesiod and the old
Cyclic poets, and the new lyricism
That had taken over. But if he failed, he failed

By being monolithic in a time of schism.
In him the epic grew smaller and the lyric grew larger.
He catches the light of the past and the future like a prism.

Rooted in the heroic past, he was a searcher
For new forms, new rhythms, and new ideas,
A poet, a musician, and a teacher.

Ibycus came from Rhegium, where the heirs
Of the Dorians and the Ionians lived together,
But when he placed himself under the laws

Of Samos, Polycrates having called him thither
To be a colleague of Anacreon,
His poetry changed with the changing of the weather

And he began to write in the Aeolian
Tradition, his poems becoming more subjective
And more erotic until his reputation

As a male Sappho quite eclipsed the fictive
Epico-lyrics of his earlier period.
Love strikes at me, he said, like the vindictive

Rush of the Thracian blast, when the lightnings add
Fire to the wind, shaking the heart to pieces.
This happens to me all the year round, he said,

Not just in April, when the holy quinces
Turn green in Athena's garden, being watered
By little streams that, wrinkled by the breezes,

Are led in ditches from the river, and scattered
Among the grape vines. When I see love coming, he said,
I shake like an old war horse when the war cry's uttered.

Simonides came from Ceos where the law required
That when a man reached sixty he should drink
Hemlock. This was done to conserve food.

The poet left there in his youth (I can't think
Why all the inhabitants didn't do the same)
And went to Athens, then tottering on the brink

Of revolution, found shelter in the home
Of Hipparchus, but after he was killed
He praised his host's murderer in a poem,

For money. He was witty, worldly, and skilled
Beyond all others in the epigram.
The epitaph he wrote for the Spartans felled

At Thermopylae dignifies his name
Beyond all human weakness: STRANGER, GO
AND TELL THE LACEDAIMONIANS AT HOME

THAT WE LIE HERE, BECAUSE THEY TOLD US TO.
Being aphoristic, he was often quoted.
He was the very laureate of woe,

Pulling out all the stops, and he was noted
For pulling his punches, as the wind shifted,
And being very careful how he voted.

Pindar was a theosophist who lifted
The veil of Isis, he learned reincarnation
From Pythagoras, like Xenophanes he sifted

The ribald myths of Homer, and the Asian
Savagery of Cybele, and found them wanting,
Yet he was able to compromise with reason

To the extent of doing a bit of bacchanting.
He was as humorless as Dante or Milton,
And just as great. He used his greatness chanting

The glory of boys who were racing mules, or belting
The daylights out of each other. He learned his craft
From Lasus, but when he became too prodigal, pelting

His hearers with too much opulence, was rebuffed
By Corinna, who told him: SOW WITH THE HAND, NOT THE SACK.
A proud and lonely thinker who seldom laughed,

Politically a middle-of-the-track,
He wrote poetry while Aeschylus was fighting
At Salamis and Marathon, but he had luck

And Athens gave him ten thousand drachmas for writing
A dithyramb in which he praised her cause.
A marble poet, superb and uninviting.

Bacchylides is not great enough to have flaws.
Humane, mundane, lacking intensity,
Polished and fluent, languid and full of grace,

He is always ready to have a good cry
Over the passing of youth and the passing of life.
He was Simonides' nephew, in his day

A better poet, but Pindar thought it safe
To call them both crows and himself an eagle,
Though either one of them would furnish tough

Competition to later poets. Now the regal
Line was drawing to an end. The Greek genius
Had said its say in the lyric. A new vehicle,

The drama, had taken its place, and the old Silenus
Who asked men questions that they couldn't answer,
Sitting under the plane tree with the contentious

Athenian boys, their thoughts leaping like a dancer
Between the swords, had made men's minds too curious
For art that didn't at least attempt to answer

Questions that stung like gadflies. It was a serious
Age. The human mind almost won out,
But not quite. It went down swinging, in the hilarious

Old Comedy. Its last word was a shout.

VIII

There are no leaves left
On the maple.
The grey November rain
Has taken them all off.

My dreams were troubled last night.
This is more than the end of the year.
It is the end of an age.
It is the end of an age of ages.

When language is despised
And words are no longer respected
The world spirit goes back to its cave
Like a woodchuck frightened by its shadow.

PART TWO

I

Who walks on the waters
Over the heads of the sulphur-bottom, the blue whale,
The bottle-nose, the cachelot, the giant squid,
The octopus, made famous by Victor Hugo,
The nautilus, celebrated by Dr. Holmes and Miss Moore.

Around his feet, barking like puppies,
Play porpoise and dolphin, dugong and the maned
Manatee, mistaken for mermaids
By mythopoeic mariners,
Sea otters, sea lions, sea cows, and the sea elephant
Rendered illustrious by Dr. Williams.

Around his head wheel cormorants and boobies,
Terns, gannets, pouched pelicans,
Man-o-war birds, petrels and flying fish.
Penguins with vestigial wings cut the water
In circles about him, and high above him veers
The albatross, made familiar to all by Coleridge.

Hagfish and lampreys surround him,
Loggerheads lumber after him,
Batfish and goosefish swim beside him
Waving lighted lanterns, which dangle
From long stalks that grow out of their heads,
A phenomenon first observed by Aristotle.

Creatures without locomotion look up as he goes by:
Mussels, abalones, quahogs,
Corals and barnacles. Gulfweeds
Wave before him like Palm Sunday.
Oysters offer him their pearls,
Something that has never been reported before by anybody.

Waves lower their whitecaps before him.
Icebergs crack, making a noise like thunder,
Melted by his love.
The winds curl up at his feet like cats.
Lord, if it be thou,
Bid me come unto thee on the water.

IV

Hearing Della Casa sing, my thoughts go back
To singers who have been silent a long time:
   Dedu-Min, whose singing delighted
   The king, and the female singer Khuyet.

They played the grave music of the Old Kingdom
On harps of five strings. They are playing it still
   On the wall of Antefoker's tomb
   At Thebes, but silently, but silently.

VIII

I saw the great cities of Warsaw and Budapest
The beautiful
The wonders of the west
And the woeful
Ruin and rubble of them, and I heard a voice crying
Weep for the cities of Warsaw and Budapest
For Moscow and New York
For London, Paris and Rome,
And for the golden cities of the east,
Rangoon, Bangkok, Peking,
Weep for them and for the stinking
Ash heaps where they stood
Where they went up in smoke spotting the earth's skin
White with the leprosy of man.

X

The Hardanger violin
With eight strings,
Four of them sympathetic,
Retains a vestigial existence
Among the Norwegians of North Dakota

With whom also persists
The terrible Halling,
Now become a dance
For athletes, in which
Nobody gets knifed any more.

PART THREE

I

Veni Creator Spiritus
Who moved upon the face of the waters
When the gases liquified
Slowly, and into the boiling ocean
Meteors, planetesimals and asteroids
Fell with a hissing plop
Augmenting the earth's mass.
Then continents rose out of the cooling water,
Lava poured from craters,
Rain fell, rivers carried sediments
To the sea turning salt.

Life was born fathoms down. It took a long time:
Carbon atoms forming in chains, like necklaces,
Water membranes fitting snug around colloids,
Droplets of coazervate splitting in two,
Iron and sulphur bacteria feeding by oxidation
And other bacteria devouring organisms,
These things went on for hundreds of millions of years
Before the exquisite algae were born, and the huge
Cambrian worms dragged along the wet sand
Which hardened to sandstone, preserving their tracks forever
In geometric beauty,

Before the armored trilobite, terrible as a tank,
Cruised the ocean bottom. Millepedes and scorpions,
Escaping to dry land, remained there
Among the expatriate seaweeds: giant horsetails,
Club mosses and ferns. But certain worms,
Instead of clothing themselves in armor like the trilobite,
Developed an internal spine. These became fish,
Amphibians, reptiles, birds, mammals, primates,

Apes, hominids, and man, the first creature
To whom it was given to decide his own future,
And he chose to die.

IV

In my third book I extolled
        the late predynastic ostrich vases,
But the middle predynastic, with palm trees,
        are no less beautiful.

VIII

The beautiful expression
'Cut from the living rock'
Always puzzled me, for rock is not living.
But now, having seen the mountains of the west,
                the buttes and the mesas,
Living their own life, unsubdued to man's use,
I understand the words.
For this city is full of rock,
The streets are made of it, the pavements and the buildings,
But it is no longer living,
It is ground into the fabric
Of a civilization
Dying of an unclean disease
Like an old nag half gone with the bots.

PART TWO

Japan

1953–1994

from

SEVENTY POEMS

(PART TWO)

(1965)

IN YOKOHAMA HARBOR

What am I doing here,
where my people unleashed
the age of horror

sowing the plague
that will kill us all?
Can I be loved?

Is it possible
this earth will not scorch
the soles of my feet?

Lord Buddha and Lord Christ
help me to walk
lightly on this soil.

THE GREAT BUDDHA AT KAMAKURA

The first thing I saw in the station was: JAPAN'S GREATEST
      JAZZ COMBO
AT THE BUDDHA HOTEL, KAMAKURA.
I had been sure of what I was getting into,
But now I was surer.
I walked the whole distance, after all
I was on pilgrimage.
As I entered the precincts I heard 'I Went To Your Wedding'
Sung by Patti Page,
And there it was, as I had dreamed of seeing it
Since I was a boy:
Plunged in unplummetted peace, invulnerable
To sorrow and joy.
People were milling around the bars
And the soft drinks houses.
There were hundreds of students all over the place,
The boys in their uniforms and the girls in their blouses,
Definitely on holiday, but well behaved
And as solemn as owls.
My heart yearned over them all, as if they were
The children of my own bowels.
Then people began to leave. The place became empty and silent
As the sun went down.
Birds alighted on the Buddha's head, roosting there in a circle
Like a halo or a crown.

THE ROCK GARDEN AT RYOANJI

This is the ultimate subtlety of art,
The marrow in the bones:
A rectangle of raked gravel
And a few stones.

AT HIROSHIMA

When we came out of the station
The houses looked old, and we wondered.

But after we had walked for a while
We came to a place with wide streets

And all the buildings were new.
Children were playing on the sidewalks,

Crying to each other in shrill voices.
Bicycles went by, jingling their bells.

But we knew we were standing
Where the end of the world began.

KATSURA IMPERIAL VILLA

Americans can see a Mondrian
But Japanese can live in one.
That is why they do not care at all
To put one on the wall.

SAIDAIJI

The eleven headed Kannon at Saidaiji
towers to the roof
like the Athene Parthenos.

But Kannon holds in her hands
a vase in which she collects
the tears of the sorrowful.

Athene carried spear and shield.
She was the goddess of wisdom
and cared nothing for tears.

THE NINTH SYMPHONY AT TAKARAZUKA

Nothing has changed. This is where I have always been.
This is where I am, wherever I go.
Nothing else matters. Let everything betray me,
In this there is no shadow of turning.

SUZUMUSHI

The suzumushi's name means 'bell insect.'
Now, in September,
They sing in my garden, in a cage
Replenished with tomato and cucumber.

They eat their husbands. Like everything else, they have
Their saturnalia and their hells.
All night I lie and listen to their song
Like little silver bells.

NARA

Over the Nara hills the October sky
Is grey and cold.
Under my window lies the holy city,
More than twelve centuries old.

Around the hotel the autumn wind wails
Continually.
The room is chilly, winter is closing in,
But all is well with me.

SOUNDS

To me the sound of falling rain
Is very beautiful,
But Japanese prefer the sound of snow
Which I can't hear at all.

GOOD MORNING

Squatting over a hole in the floor
during my matutinal defecation
I was startled to observe
regarding me through the open window

the fawn-like face
of the young gardener at Kinkakuji
who had come to collect that
to which at the moment I was contributing.

In my difficult position
I attempted a bow
saying,
Ohayo gozaimasu

which is, being interpreted,
Good morning
or (somewhat more literally)
It is an honorable earliness.

CRICKET

I found a cricket in my bedroom
but I chose to ignore it.

The next night it was still there,
looking, I thought, rather dejected.

I caught it in a handkerchief
and put it outdoors.

All that night
it sang under my window.

A STUDENT WHO SAT FACING ME
ON THE OSAKA EXPRESS

Under his persistent look I closed my eyes,
pretending to doze.

When I opened them he was still staring
so I resumed the pose.

Sitting there with closed eyes, I thought:
Look your fill.

I have no defences left
and no concealment. I am what you see,

an old man, twisted and ugly,
and as unconcerned as a tree.

KYOTO

Coming home in a taxi
after the day's heat
the cool air poured in the window

and over the city in the west
Venus and the new moon
brighter than I had ever seen them.

There is no end, I said,
of love and beauty
and fulfillment,

and my dust
will be a part of Japan
forever.

from

AUTOBIOGRAPHY (1971)

Je ne sais pas de qui je suis la proie.
Je ne sais pas de qui je suis l'amour.

AUTOBIOGRAPHY IN FIFTY SENTENCES

1. I am a New England Puritan.

2. My family came from Ipsley which is five miles from Stratford-upon-Avon.

3. My seven times great grandfather Thomas Hooker who founded Hartford where I was born was the father of American Congregationalism.

4. Mrs. Lydia Sigourney lived next door to us.

5. That was before my time though.

6. Mrs. Sigourney died in 1865 and Mr. Hubbell was born in 1901 so the rumors implying an adulterous connection between them are totally unsubstantiated.

7. Onaip is piano spelled backwards.

8. The first sentence I ever read was 'I can see you.'

9. That was in the first grade of the West Middle grammar school when I was six.

10. The first movie I ever saw was called *What Americans are made of.*

11. It was about a little boy who was left alone in the house and a burglar came in and he held the burglar at bay with a rifle until his parents came home.

12. That is what Americans are made of.

13. The first play I ever saw was called *Black Beauty.*

14. They had a real horse on the stage.

15. The first time I saw Pauline Frederick she was sitting on a camel.

16. A dromedary, not a cigarette.

17. She was the most beautiful woman I have ever seen.

18. When I was eight we moved to Kenyon Street.

19. The rockers of rocking chairs are called Basley snakes.

20. I have no idea how that got in.

21. November 1923: non posso dicer di lei quello che mai non fue detto d'alcuna.

22. From 1925 to 1946 I lived in New York.

23. Of those twenty one years I remember only Duchamp, Brancusi, Malevich, and Mondrian.

24. My family was refined we never said shit, we said Number Two.

25. From 1946 to 1953 I lived in Hartford, Connecticut.

26. Number Two on Hartford, Connecticut.

27. I left Hartford forever on August 20, 1953.

28. 'Vomiting out of the train window,' to quote Stephanie Terenzio.

29. The Japanese are just as lousy.

30. But oh the difference to me.

31. I spent that weekend in the Catskills.

32. My last night in San Francisco I saw Simionato make her American debut in Werther.

33. I arrived in Japan on October 6, 1953.

34. I arrived in Kyoto on October 9, 1953.

35. I saw my first Nō drama on October 21, 1953.

36. It was Kongō Iwao in *Fuji Daiko*.

37. There are 240 Nō plays in the classic repertory.

38. At this writing I have seen 180 of them.

39. This is my autobiography.

40. Ezra Pound spells it Noh.

41. I saw Hashi Yukio for the first time in 1960.

42. That was the same year I was naturalized.

43. I take refuge in the Buddha.

44. I take refuge in the Doctrine.

45. I take refuge in the Order.

46. You'd die laughing if you knew some of the things I've taken
    refuge in.

47. I read Shakespeare every day.

48. I read Ibsen every year.

49. The supreme moment of the twentieth century is Dorothy Mac-
    Gowan singing 'Animal crackers in my soup.'

50. En ceste foy je vueil vivre et mourir.

ROUGH CROSSING

A rough crossing. It was rough all the way,
Wind shrieking in the shrouds,
The decks awash, and there was hardly a day
The sun was not hidden by clouds.

More than once I was given up for dead,
Listed among the lost,
But I always knew that there was land ahead,
And now I have crossed.

from

CLIMBING TO MONFUMO (1977)

CLIMBING TO MONFUMO

Climbing to Monfumo
The flanks of the hill were covered with blossoming peach
And the frail almond,
But when I had reached the little church on the summit
There was nothing beyond but the Grappa,
Covered with snow although it was mid April.

Climbing to Monfumo
I remembered the greatness of these hills
When Cornaro tittered with Bembo, and Ezzelino before them,
But in the shadow of the Grappa I remembered you and your pride
And the greatness of my own days.

KAMAKURA
(1967)

After fourteen years the loud speaker blaring jazz had gone.
The bars and the soft drink stalls had gone with time.
The G.I. whores who climbed on the statue to be photographed
Were superseded by a sign that said: DO NOT CLIMB

ON THE STATUE. Japan had reasserted itself.
Reverence had returned to the place.
But to the Buddha it was as if nothing had happened.
There was no change in his face.

YAMATO

At Amagasaki in Osaka-fu one village
and in Azuchimachi, Shiga-ken, one more
have slept through twenty-one centuries of tillage
in times of peace, and of pillage
in times of war.

On the calends of January in 104
(B.C.) Jugurtha was dragged in chains
at the chariot wheels of Marius before
being thrust beneath the prison floor
where starvation ended his pains

and in the summer of 102
at Aquae Sextiae
Marius slew
two hundred thousand Teutones who
were looking for homes. At Vercellae

the following year
one hundred thousand Cimbri
were killed, drawn up in a hollow square
and tied together with ropes. Rome paid dear
for this in the fifth century.

Meanwhile in 81
at Praeneste
Sulla had twelve thousand men
slain
in one day

and during his proscriptions
in Rome
four thousand seven hundred noble Romans
were executed. For the humans
living around Lake Biwa and those whose home

was on Osaka Bay
things were quiet enough:
fishing, making clay
pots and haniwa during the day,
and at night making love.

KOCHI

In the mountains of Kochi-ken
Hirata Motome found some Ordovician
Fossil mollusks, from the time when
Shikoku was under the ocean.

In the museum at Godaisan
They lie in a row,
That were, four hundred million years ago,
Alive as we are now.

WELCOME GUESTS

Having lived for seventeen years in a house
Swarming with centipedes, millepedes, flying ants,
Cockroaches, mosquitoes, and carrion flies,
I have at last found shelter in a brand new
Ferro-concrete apartment house, with metal screens
At every window. Now my only guests
Are innocuous and charming.

When autumn comes the spiders appear.
In Japan all spiders are harmless.
They are reticent, they never get *on* you.
Furthermore, they eat flies and mosquitoes,
Which are not harmless.

Also in autumn come the crickets.
I found a baby cricket sliding helplessly
Along the sides of my stainless steel sink.
I caught it and dropped it among the leaves
Of the willow that brushes my kitchen window.

Occasionally a ladybug strolls across my desk.
They are tame and climb nonchalantly onto my outstretched finger,
Which enables me to carry them to the window
And let them fly away.

Thus by a change of habitat have I been metamorphosed
From a mass murderer
Into a gracious host.

SUNDAY AFTERNOON

Needing to be alone,
I put a sign on my gate:
Have gone to Nara. Return
Sunday night.

During the afternoon
I heard some one come,
Hesitate, then walk away.
The footsteps sounded reluctant and slow.
Whoever it was, I let him go.

MISSA SOLEMNIS

Attending a performance
Of the Missa Solemnis
At Kosei Nenkin Kaikan
In Osaka,
It was not an outstanding performance,
The soprano had a wicked tremolo, there were the usual
Bloopers in the brass, but suddenly,
As I listened to the music of Beethoven
And the words of the Mass,
I thought:

This could not have evolved from carbon compounds
And colloids. There must be something else
Involved in all this.

MATSUE

the bridge at Matsue
in the cool night

the boat lanterns
moving silently

NOVA SCOTIA

These islands were struck from obsidian
With two harsh blows, and left. They did not spring
Like flowers out of water, opening
To light as islands in other bays have done.
The evergreen, the bunchgrass, and the moss,
The maple and the oak, the slaty shale
In this grey northern fishing town prevail
Instead of the hibiscus and the rose.

In this invulnerable landscape without heart
I am a guest. No part of it is mine.
The Scotland blue spruce and the Norway pine
Are passionless, perfected, set apart.
Now all things vehement and all things dear
Are far away. I am an orphan here.

NEANDERTAL

The neandertal, more sensitive
Than any ape, not quite a man,
Had intimations of art.

He chose, to fashion tools from,
Caught by their beauty,
Rock crystal and Spanish topaz.

Blunted bits of manganese,
Faceted with use, betray
That he painted his body.

Even the proto-neandertal
Of the Riss-Würm deposit
Cherished the cave bear's jaw

Bearing the fortuitous look
Of a man's head, in profile,
Which he wore as a fetish.

Later, to increase the likeness,
He would bore a hole
Where the eye should be.

LIT'RY QUATRAINS

1

Man's time on earth is quickly sped
While jewels have a life aeonian.
Beautiful Evelyn Hope is dead
But the Hope Diamond is in the Smithsonian.

2

Gabriel Harvey's hexameters Thomas Nash wittily mimics,
Setting the fashion for subsequent tribes of insensitive critics.
Saintsbury, wittiest of scholars, perceived they were meant to be funny.
It was unlikely the comrade of Spenser should be such a ninny.

3

Whitman's views on poetry
Were frequently profound,
But where music and painting were concerned
He didn't know his ass from a hole in the ground.

4

Darwin, Frazer, Marx, and Freud
Are writers no one should avoid,
But for cleaning out our attics
There's nothing like the pre-Socratics.

5

In youth our hearts are supersonic
And easily become Platonic
But when we've passed our perihelions
We freeze into Aristotelians.

6

When poetry was on the wane,
Blighted by the Christian bane,
Nonnus gave an epic squeak
And wrote the longest poem in Greek.

7

Webster, Tourneur, Ford, and Shirley
Are full of turgid hurly-burly.
I must confess that I prefer
The clarity of Massinger.

8

Pierre Loti lived in many lands and wrote
Of obscure places and exotic lairs.
Emily Dickinson sat at her desk
And wouldn't come downstairs.

9

People who talk about Dear Jane
Give me (you know where) a pain.
I love Maria Edgeworth dearly.
She's just as good as Jane, or nearly.

JACK JOHNSON

Jack Johnson is dead. He wasn't a good nigger.
To him white women were just like other women,
White men were just like any other men,
Which didn't go down so good.

Jack Johnson was a leopard, a panther, a big cat,
He moved like music and he hit like atoms,
But he never could learn to say Yassuh Mistah Boss,
Which didn't contribute to his popularity.

Jack Johnson had to take it on the lam
When he got in trouble over a white woman
So they paid him to take a dive for Jess Willard
And he ended up lecturing in a flea circus.

I met Jack Johnson once. He was intelligent
But he never could seem to learn to know his place.
God bless him, wherever he is.
He never kissed a white ass in his life.

THE ROAD NOT TAKEN

One night I was reading in bed,
In the house of my childhood.
I was about sixteen
And was reading a Buddhist book.
Suddenly I realized what it was all about:
Give up all desires. Renounce everything.
I approached the abyss. I looked into it.
I turned back in terror. The moment passed.
It never came again.
I had missed it, for this life.

NATURE

Nature cleans up after herself,
Jane Heap used to say.
We see evidence of this
Every day

As by pollution, over-population,
And nuclear war,
The 'odious race of vermin' is exterminating itself
From this unhappy star.

Soon there will be nothing but rock,
Sand
(Which is pulverized rock),
And

Water: but there's a fearful thought.
Life begins in water. Suppose,
After a million years of cleansing,
Once more in the seas,

Carbon compounds and colloids
Start all over again
The evolutionary process
That leads to man,

Until anew
Homo sapiens stands erect, the process completed,
Murderous and cretinous,
And the whole shabby farce is repeated.

IT WON'T BE LONG NOW

Every baby that is born
Brings the end nearer.

Every automobile that is bought
Brings the end nearer.

But nobody cares.
The human race

Is like a cloud of midges
Swarming in summer sunshine,

So brief,
So brainless.

DE SENECTUTE

1

When I was young and derogate
My lineaments were adequate,
But now that I have learned to conster
I find myself become a monster.

2

I'd rather look
The way I do
Than be what I was
When I looked better.

LADYBUG

The orange wings with black dots, folding,
Meet cleanly with sharp edges
Joined perfectly, fitting your
Body like a shield.

Your progress across my hand
Is singularly inoffensive
Considering that I am not as a rule
Partial to insects.

When I have opened the screen door
And extended my arm,
The neat case becomes a sudden
Whir, like a hummingbird.

THE DEATH OF THE CACTUS

For seven years this little plant
Grew, austere and elegant.
For five days I watched it shrink,
Turn grey, refuse to drink,
Then go from one small pot of loam
Back to the universe, its home.

from

WALKING THROUGH NAMBA (1978)

WALKING THROUGH NAMBA

Walking through Namba in the still air
Of early day,
On my way
To the Shin Kabuki-za, and nearly there,

I found myself saying a sonnet, learned long ago,
By Hildegarde Flanner.
In gentle manner
The words came back to me, hesitant and slow,

And as I approached the theatre all desire
In me was dead,
And I said,
'How mystical my flesh and without fire.'

JAINS

The Jains are forbidden to injure any living thing,
moving or unmoving: the latter refers to plants.

Roots, bulbs, tubers, anything that grows underground
is prohibited. To eat a root you must destroy the life of the plant.

Potatoes, carrots, parsnips, turnips, radishes, onions, beets,
all interdicted, but in their stead what a feast is spread before them:

fruits from the tree, berries from the bush, nuts from the vine,
beans and corn from the stalk,

and heavier things that grow along the ground:
melons of all kinds, gourds and cucumbers, pumpkins and squash.

Today the world has been inherited by
the torturer, the terrorist, the assassin.

In such a world, imagine being able to say:
No potato has died because of me.

AT KANRYUJI

Sitting on the steps of Kanryuji, on a hill overlooking Kurashiki, on
a perfect autumn day, not a cloud in the sky, complete silence among
the stone images and the enormous trees, except for the crying of the
crows, I reflected on the fact that seventy six years had brought me to
this spot, from the other side of the world, and I thought of the spot
where I was born, a house in Hartford

> when I was eight
> they tore it down
> to build a high school
>
> fifty years later
> they tore down the high school
> to make a cloverleaf
>
> (so I am told,
> though I have no idea
> what a cloverleaf is)
>
> but long before that
> I had escaped
> to New York
>
> and from thence
> to Kyoto
> and finally to Kobe
>
> and I said to myself:
> There is something
> that is taking care of me.

OCEAN

Every year, as soon as school closed,
when I was a boy, we loaded up the car
and headed for our summer home
on Long Island Sound.

Every year, at about the same place,
my mother would lift her head, sniff, and cry out,
The ocean! Smell it! I can smell the ocean!
We all sniffed,

and there it was, unmistakable,
the clean salt smell of the sea,
although the shore was still
miles ahead of us.

All that was sixty years ago,
and more. I wonder what it smells like now,
the ocean a garbage dump, slimy with oil,
fish dying by the billion,

and the silver footed mother of Achilles,
with the other daughters of Nereus,
lying in their cave, tettered over
with the leprosy of man.

CONVERSATION IN GION

Good evening, Uncle.
Good evening.
Do you want a girl, Uncle?
Not particularly.
Do you want a boy, Uncle?
Not particularly.
Do you want marijuana, Uncle?
Not particularly.
What *do* you want, Uncle?
I'm just taking a walk. I like to walk.
Have a nice walk, Uncle.

PUERTO RICO

At the hotel in Santurce
All the room boys were whores.
They would lay for anyone,
Male or female,

All except Andréas
Who was proud and scornful
And wore a baseball cap
On the back of his head.

MUSICAL INSTRUMENTS

The organ in Convention Hall
at Atlantic City
has 32,882 pipes,
1,233 stops,
and 7 keyboards.

The *ichi-gen-kin*
has one string.

That is why
I do not believe
in progress.

TREE

Like fruit from a shaken tree
my beliefs have fallen from me.

Like leaves before a gust
they lie scattered in the dust.

After the autumn rains
only the trunk remains.

from

THE FIRST ARCHITECT (1982)

NOTE

In *The First Architect* the title poem appears as the book's second piece (after 'At 80'). It was originally published in *Seventy Poems* (1965); in this *Selected Poems* it is printed in its original context on pages 148-49.

AT 80

I know many things,
but not what I would most
like to know.

A Nativity Play

The action takes place in the ocean.

    First Diatom
Wei-la, wei-la,
A-la-la, a-la-la,
Wei-la, wei-la.

    Second Diatom
What the hell are you supposed to be?
One of the Rhine Maidens?

    First Diatom
A-la-la, a-la-la,
Wei-la, wei-la …

    Third Diatom
Oh, come off it, will you?

    First Diatom
I am no ordinary alga.
I am an artist.
The basso rilievo where my valves are joined
Has been compared
To the Apollonian pediment at Olympia.

    Second Diatom
My God, she's been reading Hubbell …

BACTERIA

The bacteria are in a drop of water
under a microscope and their enlarged image
projected on a screen that we may witness
the bacterial ballet

of flagellate Nijinskies, coccus Kreutzbergs,
actinomycete Isadoras, and the
exquisite cladothrix, like Ruth St. Denis
as Isis or Kwannon.

FOR THE EMPEROR'S 77TH BIRTHDAY

The long grasses of Sagami Bay
Wave slowly in the tide.
The fish dart on their secret errands,
The crabs teeter on spindly legs.
The sea-anemones bloom
In the deep gardens of the ocean.

REMEMBERING TESHIMA-SENSEI

How simple a truly great artist can be!

For fifteen years Sensei and I were neighbors,
And when we met on the densha he would bow,
Saluting me like an old gentleman from the country.
At such times I used to think:
What depths beyond depths of wisdom and creative power
Are lying there, perfectly relaxed,
In that man who, to an idle eye,
Might be an old farmer.

I cherish these memories
Now that his wisdom and his greatness
Have become a part of the universe.

QUESTION

A current
goes through a wire.

Am I the current?
or the wire?

My future
depends on that.

CHIBA-KEN

In Chiba-ken, at Kanzaki-machi,
under the Nishinojo Shell Mound,
a pit-dwelling nine thousand years old
was found

containing the lovely Igusa pottery
on which the lines are cut
with rushes, not ropes as in the Jomon.
At the bottom of the pit

the earth was packed hard
by the treading of many feet,
as around the bison
of Tuc d'Audoubert the footprints

of Magdalenian dancers
are preserved to this day.
Footprints outlast the feet,
and clay survives the clay.

A POEM ABOUT JAPAN

On Sunday in Kurashiki
walking through busloads of Japanese tourists,
looking at the groups plodding through the museum,
following their guide like cattle,
seeing nothing and caring for nothing,
and the high school girls
giggling in front of the El Greco and the Cezannes,
I said to myself:
No country in the world
is as vulgar as Japan.

Then I turned into a side street
and from the second floor of an old house
I heard voices singing *Hagoromo* . . .
Azuma Asobi no kazu kazu ni . . .
and I knew that they were a group of young men
who come there every Sunday to sing yōkyoku
for their pleasure,
and I said to myself:
No country in the world
is as refined as Japan.

PEBBLES

These two pebbles from Miho no Matsubara,
        so marvelously shaped
by the immemorial sculpture of the ocean,
antedating by a billion years
the architecture of the diatom
and the mimesis of the annelata,
surviving the shock and shifting of continents,
abraded by wind and water and lava flood,
lie here at last on my desk, perfect works of art.
Only Brancusi could have made anything as beautiful.

SOUVENIR DE VOYAGE

The morning after Honolulu
I came out on deck
before breakfast

and there to starboard
was a mountain-high cone of rock,
obviously uninhabited.

When I came back on deck
after breakfast
it was gone.

Then for eight days
nothing but scooped wave
and thrown spray

and on the ninth
I came out on deck
before breakfast

and there to larboard,
shining in the morning dusk,
the lights of Miura Hanto.

MERRIE ENGLAND

In London's fair city, where girls are so pretty,
And the University Wits are so witty,
Poets, scholars, and men of distinction
Are gathered to witness a bear's extinction.

The bear is destroyed in the drollest way:
His eyes are put out, and when he can't see
He is tied to the wall with a heavy chain
While five or six men bash out his brain.

That's all the performance consists of.
To you it may seem simple enough,
But great minds often find relaxation
In the simplest forms of recreation.

After all, you don't have a chance every day
To see the charred flesh crumble away
From the bones of a woman who's burning alive.
(There's nothing to equal the screams *they* give.)

Hey nonny nonny and down a down derry,
The sun is a-setting on Twickenham Ferry.
Winter or summer, spring or fall,
Simple pleasures are best of all.

LOVE SONG

My beloved is fair faced
And beautiful behinded,
But absent minded.

All day I pick up things
Meticulously misplaced:
Wrist watch, glasses, rings,

Notebook and coat.
I bring them back, and then
They are mislaid again.

How gladly I devote
To my distrait, my nervous,
This inconspicuous service.

HARTFORD

The skull found
in Kungwangling Hill
Lantien county
Shensi province

is said to predate
Pithecanthropus
(renamed Sinanthropus)
Pekinensis

by a thousand centuries
being thought to be
five or six hundred thousand
years old

in the meantime
Pekinensis has disappeared
having been last heard of
in America

and when I was in Hartford
they showed it at the
Museum of Natural History
in New York

and I went down to see it
and everybody roared with laughter
and said,
He's going to New York to look at a bone!

WADI EN NAR

Thirty eight years before Saint Benedict
Founded Monte Cassino, Saint Sabas
Founded a monastery in the Wadi En Nar
(Valley of Fire) in what is now Jordan.
It is still there. Ten monks live under the edict
Of the founder. They get up at 2 a.m. Being far
From electricity they have no telephone. They pass
The day with only one meal: olives and cheese
And fish. They drink rain water. A half hour before sunset
They go to bed. They have laid down the burden.
War rages around them. They are at peace,
Praying, meditating, doing the chores, they do not fret
At sonic booms or the noise of an occasional jet.
In a mad world they are sane, their minds at ease.

ONE LINE OF POETRY

(April 3, 1936)

The night Hauptmann was killed
I walked the streets of New York all night

(in those days one could walk New York streets at night
without being mugged or murdered)

believing him innocent,
picturing the horror of the electrocution,
I could not stay in my room
and walked the streets for hours.

God knows I didn't think of writing poetry,
but one line kept coming persistently into my mind:

Out of the sty. Well out, and cleanly out.

In forty six years I have never written that down.
In forty six years I have never forgotten it.

Now that his name is being cleared
I write it down for the first time
and lay it on his dishonored grave.

SUWA JINJA

Two hundred and twenty nine
stone steps

not bad for an old guy
of eighty one

at the top
silence

mountains of green
blue beyond

not even out of breath
I called aloud

on the helpers and servers
of Master Builder Solness

for help
in my new life.

WAKA

I am not a person.
I am a succession of persons
Held together by memory.

When the string breaks,
The beads are scattered.

NOTES

NOTES

THE NINTH PLANET

A hypothetical planet beyond Neptune whose existence would help to explain oddities in the orbits of some bodies in the extreme outer reaches of the solar system. Its existence was first hypothesised in 1906; in 1930 astronomer Clyde Tomball discovered Pluto, which was at first taken to be the ninth planet although it was later judged to be too small to qualify as a true planet.

HENRIK IBSEN

While working on *The Master Builder*, Ibsen spent some time at the Tyrolean resort of Gossensass. While there he met Emilie Bardach, an eighteen-year-old student from Vienna, with whom he had a brief affair. *An die Maisonne eines Septemberlebens* [To the May-sun of a September-life] is the dedicatory inscription on the back of a photograph which Ibsen gave to Emilie when they parted; it is dated 27 September 1889. It has been claimed that Bardach was the model for Hilda in the play. That summer, Ibsen also met Helene Raff, a friend of Bardach's, who told him the story of a builder who fell to his death from the tower of his recently completed building.

CITY OF ISLANDS

Hubbell attended Constantin Brancusi's second New York solo exhibition at the Wildenstein Gallery in 1926.

FIVE PLACES

Charles Sheeler (1883–1965): American modernist artist and photographer, who often painted urban landscapes and industrial scenes.

Amphitrite: goddess of the sea, consort of Poseidon.

GREENPOINT VIII: *En ce temps-là le désert était peuplé d'anachorètes* [In those days there were many anchorites living in the desert]: the first sentence of *Thaïs* (1890), a novel by Anatole France set in fourth-century Egypt.

RIDGEWOOD IV: Walter Conrad Arensberg (1878–1954): American art collector, critic and poet. He and his wife Louise were close friends and life-long patrons of Marcel Duchamp; when Duchamp's *Fountain* was rejected for the first show of the Society of Independent Artists in New York in 1917, Arensberg resigned from the society in protest. He and his wife left New York and moved permanently to Hollywood in 1921.

RIDGEWOOD VII: *Stell auf den Tisch die duftenden Reseden* [Place on the table the fragrant mignonettes]: the first line of 'Allerseelen' [All Souls' Day], a poem by Herman von Gilm, set by Richard Strauss in 1885, op. 10, no. 8.

THE FIRST ARCHITECT

Rudolph Bauer (1889–1953): German non-objective (abstract) painter associated with the avant-garde *Der Sturm* group. He emigrated to America in 1939.

JACQUES VACHÉ

Jacques Vaché (1885–1919): a friend of André Breton, who credited Vaché with being a major inspiration for surrealism. He died – along with a naked male companion – of an opium overdose in a hotel room in Nantes.

ATLANTIC TRIPTYCH

Lisa Della Casa (1929–2012): Swiss soprano who specialised in roles in the operas of Mozart and Strauss. Hubbell must have been listening to her on record as she did not make her American debut until November 1953, by which time Hubbell was in Kyoto.

Pauline Frederick (1883–1938): American stage and screen actress famous for her beauty; the play in which she entered on a live camel – 'a marvelous spectacle' according to Frederick's biographer, Muriel Elwood – was *Joseph and His Brethren* by Louis N. Parker, which opened at the Century Theatre in New York in January 1913. Elwood goes on: 'The camel was magnificently caparisoned, with a beautifully embroidered basourah' from which Frederick emerged, wearing a costume that 'displayed her wonderful figure in all its grace and charm' (Elwood, *Pauline Frederick: On and Off the Stage*, 54-55). Hubbell would have been eleven years old when he saw this.

November 1923: in the surviving five-page fragment of a 278-page autobiography destroyed by Hubbell in 1950, he said, 'The person I have loved most in my life was Eleanora Duse.' November 1923 was when Hubbell saw her at the start of her final American tour in Ibsen's *The Lady from the Sea*, played in Italian at the Metropolitan Opera House in New York. *Non posso dicer di lei quello che mai non fue detto d'alcuna* [I cannot say about her what has never been said about anyone] is an adaptation of Dante's line about Beatrice, *io spero di dicer di lei quello che mai non fue detto d'alcuna* [I hope to say about her what has never been said about anyone]. According to *Time* (12 November 1923), Duse held the audience 'breathless through four long acts.'

Stephanie Terenzio (1932–1999): American art critic and curator, native of Hartford.

Giulietta Simionato (1910–2010): Italian mezzo-soprano.

Kongō Iwao (1924–1998): the 25th-generation Grand Master of the Kongō school of nō in Kyoto.

Hashi Yukio (1943–): Japanese pop star singing modern enka; see the introduction, page 47.

En ceste foy je vueil vivre et mourir [In this faith I wish to live and die]: 'Ballade pour prier Nostre Dame' in section LXXXIX of Villon's *Le Testament*.

Monfumo: a village in northern Italy near Asolo, the town where Eleanora Duse's grave is located. Hubbell visited the area during his recuperative trip to Italy in 1935; in the surviving fragment of his autobiography he said that Duse loved Asolo above all other places, 'and so, at the lowest ebb of my life, it was to Asolo that I fled.'

Monte Grappa: a mountain close to Asolo. Catherine Cornaro (1454–1510) was given Asolo by the Venetians after they forced her to abdicate as Queen of Cyprus in 1489; her court, a centre of literary and artistic excellence, was the fictional setting for *Gli Asolani* [The People of Asolo], dialogues on love by Pietro Bembo (1470–1547).

Ezzelino: the Ezzelini family were the lords of the area around Asolo from 1199 on; Ezzelino III (1194–1259) was a notorious tyrant; Dante placed him in the Seventh Circle, First Ring of Hell, reserved for those violent against their neighbours (*Inferno* XII, 109).

WALKING THROUGH NAMBA

Namba: a major entertainment district in central Osaka. Shin Kabuki-za: New Kabuki Theatre.

Hildegarde Flanner (1899–1987): American poet and friend of Hubbell's; in 1981 he included four poems by her in the tenth anniversary issue of the annual *Anthology* published by Ikuta Press.

BACTERIA

Harald Kreutzberg (1902–1968): dancer with a highly expressionist style; in his lifetime the most famous German dancer.

Ruth St. Denis (1879–1968): American pioneer of modern dance who included Egyptian and Asian elements in her style; Martha Graham was her student.

Sagami Bay: a large bay south of Tokyo where warm currents from the south and cold currents from the north help create great marine biodiversity. Emperor Hirohito (Shōwa) was deeply interested in marine biology; he had a research laboratory in the Imperial Palace, published papers in the field, and discovered several new species of Hydrozoa.

REMEMBERING TESHIMA-SENSEI

Teshima Yazaemon (1899–1978): head of the Kongō school of nō and a Living National Treasure. According to the Japanese Wiki Corpus of Kyoto articles his style was 'splendid and massive with austere elegance'.

A POEM ABOUT JAPAN

Kurashiki: a town near the Seto Inland Sea in Okayama Prefecture in the west of Japan. It is famous for its many well-preserved seventeenth-century wooden warehouses, and for Japan's earliest museum of Western art, the Ōhara Museum of Art, established in 1930. The collection in-cludes both old masters and contemporary works.

Hagoromo [The Feather Mantle]: a sixteenth-century nō play with a swan-maiden motif – one of the most popular plays in the nō repertoire. The author is unknown.

Yōkyoku: the vocal part of a traditional nō play, sung by the chorus.

SOUVENIR DE VOYAGE

Miura Hanto [Miura Peninsula]: the peninsula at the south-western en-trance to Tokyo Bay, not far south of the major port of Yokohama.

WADI EN NAR

Wadi En Nar: the lower part of a valley that leads down from near the Old City of Jerusalem to the Dead Sea; the Greek Orthodox Monastery of Mar

Saba, founded in 483 CE by Saint Sabas, overlooks the valley. Saint Sabas and later monks at the monastery played important roles in the creation and preservation of the standard Byzantine Rite of the Orthodox church, and in scholarship and translation. When Hubbell wrote the poem the valley was in Jordan; since 1967 the area has been part of the occupied Palestinian territories.

ONE LINE OF POETRY

Bruno Richard Hauptmann (1899–1936): a German immigrant accused in 1932 of the kidnapping and murder of Charles Lindbergh Jr., the twenty-month-old son of the aviator Charles Lindbergh. Hauptmann's trial, which began in 1935, was highly controversial, and remained so for many years after his execution by electric chair on the date given in the poem. His last words were, *Ich bin absolut unschuldig an den Verbrechen, die man mir zur Last legt* [I am absolutely innocent of the crimes I am accused of]. His widow, Anna, fought for many years to clear his name. Her last two attempts, before her death in 1994, were in 1982 and 1986; despite Hubbell's hopeful claim in the poem, neither of these appeals was successful.

SUWA JINJA

Suwa Jinja: a major Shinto shrine in Nagasaki, famous for the long stone staircase leading up to the main buildings; Master Builder Solness is the central character in Ibsen's *The Master Builder*.

AFTERWORD

NOTE

An earlier version of Yoko Danno's memoir of Lindley Williams Hubbell was published in *The Montserrat Review* in 2009.

A MEMOIR *by* YOKO DANNO

He was like an ironstone, with the base (Western culture and literature) buried deep underground. Myself being a 'traveler' with only a small compass (intuition), and without a map, I felt sometimes a need to keep a certain distance from him so that my 'compass' wouldn't approach too near to the iron. He spurred me to write, with praises, like a good horse-trainer.

I first met Hubbell-sensei sometime in the early spring of 1967, when my professor-friend Hisao Kanaseki took me to Hubbell-sensei's semi-Western style house on the top of Kujo-yama, a hill at the eastern end of Kyoto. Kanaseki-sensei had told me that he was an accomplished poet and scholar, with piercing eyes, although he was also highly humorous. I was prepared to see a masterful professor/poet. Hubbell-sensei appeared at the door, wearing a *tanzen* [padded kimono] over a black shirt and a pair of trousers. He was stoop-shouldered, no taller than a medium-sized Japanese. He bowed deeply to us and said to me, '*kechina yaro de gozansu*' – meaning, 'I am a humble and worthless fellow,' which is a greeting that yakuza exchange at a first meeting. His dark eyes were mischievous and lively. We chatted in his living room, in the center of which was an old iron stove with a pipe going up to the ceiling. I remember he mainly talked about his life on Kujo-yama. The old house had no bath, but the *mama-san* [proprietress] of a near-by lovers' inn offered to let him use its *onsen* [hot-spring bath] late after midnight, so he went there in the early hours (his bedtime was usually 4:00, or 5:00 in the morning) and took his bath. I was thrown off my guard and my usual timidity at meeting a famed professor disappeared and I was soon relaxed.

In those days I was working on a series of poems; when I finished the first part (thirteen poems) I sent them to him. He replied: 'Your lovely *winter journey* came and I have read it several times with delight. It reminds me a little bit of 'Thirteen Ways of Looking at a Blackbird', but it is original and very beautiful.' I was easily encouraged and set out on the next series of thirteen poems, *song of destruction*, and sent him two or three poems at a time as I wrote them, to which he responded favorably, with praises. My intention was to finish a trilogy of poems as soon as possible but time lapsed with meager result, partly because I was busy taking care of my two small children, but mainly because I was at a loss about how to keep up my spirit. He kept on saying, 'Don't stop!' Then at the beginning of 1969 he wrote to me: 'You have certainly started the year not with a whimper but a bang. No. 7 (of *dance of fire*) is one of your loveliest poems.' I was spurred and finished off my first collection, *trilogy* (1970).

§

Hubbell-sensei told me in an interview with him (at Kunishima Hospital in 1994) that he began to read Shakespeare at the age of eight and had memorized all the plays by the time he was ten. His mother took him out of school to see every play of Shakespeare performed in Hartford, saying to the furious principal and teachers that it was 'more important for the boy to see Shakespeare than to come here.' Eventually he quit high school in his second year and was educated by private tutors (Greek, Latin and Provençal), and by his multilingual aunt (German, French and Italian). In his teens he saw almost all the Shakespearean performances in Hartford and New York and finally was hired by the theatrical company led by his hero actor, Robert Mantell when he was eighteen. He was given some small parts, such as Prince Edward in *Richard III*, or Balthasar in *The Merchant of Venice*, but after a year he left the company because he decided he'd rather read Shakespeare than act in it. Much later, sometime around 1976, in the tatami-room of his apartment in Kobe – where he had moved after retiring from his teaching post in Kyoto – he recited Shakespeare every Saturday evening to a small audience (his assistant Ms. Hatano, my husband and I). We called it the SSS (Saturday Shakespeare Society). It was a feast for my ears. He read Shakespeare every day until his death at the age of ninety-three.

He was one of the earliest admirers of Gertrude Stein and became a correspondent of hers and later wrote a review of the first four books of The Plain Edition of her works in 1933. When she came to New York in 1934 he saw her many times. He told me an amusing anecdote in the 1994 interview: One day she called him up and asked him to come with her to the Brooklyn Museum, where she was to give a lecture, because Alice had a cold and couldn't come. They went there in a taxi, and Gertrude introduced him to the head of the museum, saying, 'This is Alice Toklas.' He looked at Hubbell and said, 'How do you do, Miss Toklas.'

My first 'encounter' with English, as far as I remember, was when my mother put me in an English class run by an American missionary in a room of our ancestral temple. I was ten or eleven. In the room was an image of the Buddha looking down upon us from the altar. The first sentence I learned was, 'Go to the Buddha.' I was confused because the word order was completely different from Japanese, in which the order is, 'the Buddha, to, go.' Through my high school and college years I was more concerned with English grammar and sentence structure than its sounds. So when Hubbell-sensei introduced me to *Tender Buttons* I was shocked. I saw and heard English from a completely different angle, which was a wonderful and exciting experience. I felt somehow freed. He gave me as birthday presents the books of H.D., *The Handbook of Greek Mythology and Legend, The Iliad* and *The Odyssey*, among others, as well as Pound's *Cantos*, of which he said, even if you don't read it, just having it in your bookshelf is important. H.D.'s *Helen in Egypt* inspired me to write my own *Hagoromo, A Celestial Robe*, based on a legend with a swan-maiden motif recorded in the eighth century in Japan. Keeping company with Greek mythology stimulated me to translate the songs and stories of Japanese gods, goddesses, emperors and empresses of the *Kojiki* [Record of Old Matters], also compiled in the eighth century.

He actually saw and heard the celebrated artists of the West in the early twentieth century, figures whom I had only read about in a magazine, or a book, or had never heard of. In *Autobiography* he says:

> I remember what Duse sounded like when she said,
> 'Ah, Signore, datemi, voi la luce!'

> I remember what Bernhardt sounded like, when she said,
> 'Nous irons au pays du soleil.'

> I remember what Garden sounded like when she said,
> 'Il y a quelqu'n derrière nous.'

I remember what Marlowe sounded like when she said,
'And what should I do in Illyria?'

... so much else
has been forgotten

And at Kyoto Kaikan, when he was sitting in the audience who had come to see Tani Momoko in *Swan Lake*, 'suddenly the thought came to me / I am the only person here who saw Nijinsky dance.'

With him I went to many museums, galleries and exhibitions in Kyoto, Osaka and Kobe, and saw works ranging from Egyptian and Greek statues, the Mona Lisa, Rembrandt, the Impressionists, and modern paintings and sculptures, through to Independents, Happenings, and a show by a far-out artist who exhibited crumpled newspapers all over the floor. He used to say, the Japanese don't need to hang a painting by Mondrian on the wall; they live in one. He meant a Japanese house with *shōji* [lattice-framed sliding paper doors], *fusuma* [sliding paper doors inside wooden frames], wooden pillars and framed ceilings.

He hated modern technology except for his record player, which he needed in order to listen to records of his favorite music, both classical and popular. He especially hated the telephone. It's a crime to Beethoven, he said, if a telephone rings while I am listening to a record of, say, his Sixth Symphony. He came to Japan by sea and never left this country afterward.

§

Lindley Hubbell had worked as a librarian in the Map Room in the New York Public Library for twenty-one years, during which time he went to Italy and stayed there for a year, and then taught the history of drama at the Randall School of Arts in Hartford before he came to Japan in 1953. He was soon invited to teach at Dōshisha University in Kyoto. He was given the Litt.D. for his two books, *Lectures on Shakespeare* (1958) and *Shakespeare and Classic Drama* (1962).

His first five collections of poems were published in the United States between 1927 and 1965, but after the Ikuta Press was set up to bring out my *trilogy* (1970), most of Hubbell's books of poetry were published by the press, including *Autobiography* (1971), *Double Triptych* (1974), *Pasiphae* (1976), *Climbing to Monfumo* (1977), *Walking through Namba* (1978) and *The First Architect* (1982). His translations of Sophocles' *Oedipus at Colonus* (1978) and Aeschylus' *The Suppliants* (1983), together with *Translations* (1983) (from the Pyramid Texts, the *Book of the Dead*, Sappho, et al.) were also published by the Ikuta Press, which in addition brought out fourteen issues of *Anthology* (a poetry annual with Lindley Hubbell as the chief advisor) between 1972 and 1991.

He loved beautiful creations, whether natural or man-made. Here is his 'mandala' of the artists:

1. Giotto BOTTICELLI Fra Angelico REMBRANDT Canaletto Longhi Guardi Bellotto Cezanne MALEVICH Mondrian The Deluge
2. Proust Joyce Stein Pound Eliot Stevens Moore Williams Richardson H.D. The Deluge

His interest ranged wide and deep, from Egypt to Europe to America to Asia, in the mineral, plant, animal and human kingdoms alike. And he loved above all:

ENERGY

Of the unnumbered forms
That energy assumes
Three have I always loved:
Cats, cacti, and stones.

A cat can live alone
Or gracious at the hearth,
Gregarious at will,
Unmastered to the death.

The cactus grows in soil
Of little nourishment.
It thrives on what would mean
Death to another plant.

As for a stone, smothered
By the sea, and wind-scoured,
Who would not wish to be
So tempered and so hard?

Seventy Poems (1965), *Walking Through Namba* (1978)

The three things Japanese he loved most were: the nō drama; Shinto (the traditional religion of Japan); and Hashi Yukio (a Japanese pop singer). Once he was 'hooked' by beauty, he was devoted to it. He wrote:

> October 21st, 1978
> Twenty five years ago today, in the Kongō Nōgaku-dō in Kyoto, I heard for the first time, from behind the *hashigakari*, the notes of *O-shirabe*. A few minutes later I was watching my first performance of Nō: *Fuji-daiko*, with Kongō Iwao.[1]

He meticulously recorded on his list – which he titled 'Silver Anniversary' – all the nō dramas he had seen: 186 out of the 240 existing nō plays since his first viewing of nō on October 21, 1953. In all, he saw nō plays 849 times, of which he invited me to some thirty performances.

He was fascinated by the beauty of Shinto ceremonies. He wrote in a letter to me: 'Last evening I went to Kamigamo Jinja [shrine] to a lovely annual ceremony – they have thousands of *hitogata* [paper cut in a human shape] which people have brought, with their name and age written on them (and an offering, of course) and the priests strew them on a little stream which flows through the shrine. They look like flower petals on the water and the stream carries them away, carrying with them all our ills and impurities. As they floated away, the priests played Kagura [sacred Shinto music] and Gagaku [imperial court music], and all around so many people stood with joined palms, praying earnestly. Very lovely.'

Every year on the evening of the Great Festival of Kasuga in Nara, December 17, he and his close friends assembled to watch the annual offering in front of the temporary shrine built with raw timber, where

---

[1] *Nōgaku-dō* [nō-theatre]; *hashigakari* [bridge-like passsageway between backstage and stage]; *O-shirabe* [nō-music].

the young god of the Kasuga Shrine enjoys the ritual music and dance, which have been preserved since the eighth century, performed on the outdoor lawn stage.

Sensei was much older than my father but somehow we 'hit it off.' Outwardly there was nothing in common between us, except one thing: He had two names, Lindley Williams Hubbell and Hayashi Shūseki (his legal name after his naturalization in 1960) while my two names are Yoko Danno and Yoko Iida (my legal name by marriage). Outwardly we sweated and suffered, like everybody else. I lost my son on a Himalayan mountain; sensei's last years were difficult, especially the few years when he was bedridden in a hospital room shared with two or three senile patients; Sensei was the only one who was clear-headed. On Saturdays when I visited him, he was sorry he had no chair to offer me except the portable toilet. I sat on the 'chair' and soon we started chatting and forgot the morbid surroundings, absorbed in our conversation, perhaps discussing a line from Emily Dickinson, or just about flowers coming out, or about our mutual friends or my family. When I think of his 'dual' life, I am reminded of a poem in *Long Island Triptych* (1947); here are the first two stanzas:

> The heart,
> Said Rena,
> Must learn to compose, like Palestrina,
> Contrapuntally, for many voices,
> Each one a separate part,
> While one rejoices
> Another sweats in anguish.
>
> My dear,
> Said Rena,
> I suffer for you but I don't worry about you
> Because I hear
> The contrapuntal texture of your living,
> Whatever mess you are in, that goes on without you,
> Getting clearer and clearer.

And a verse written much later:

Waka

I am not a person.
I am a succession of persons
Held together by memory

When the string breaks,
The beads scatter.

And his honest notion:

At 80

I know many things,
but not what I would most
like to know.

Then his last poem (circa 1994):

having spent my life
in the service of beauty
now human garbage

§

Mrs. Ueno, the widow of the late president of Dōshisha University, who devotedly looked after him, obtained for him a private room in a Christian hospital, but he refused to move into it, saying he was dedicated to Shinto, not to Christianity. His legacy was left to Ōta Shrine in Kyoto, whose archaic music and dancing, performed by aged mediums, he especially loved.

His belief in poetry had never changed or wavered since he articulated it in the *New York Times* in 1922: 'We need not be afraid of any verse form whatever when it is in the hands of true poets. The trouble lies in the lack of whole-hearted artistic sincerity, the grotesque exaggeration of phrase, the deliberate vagueness of expression: all employed to conceal the absence of clear thinking and the inability to attain to that simplicity which is the handmaiden of beautiful language in all idioms and in all times.'

I am still on my 'journey' without a map, but the needle of my 'compass' points to the place where Lindley Williams Hubbell stands forever.